# BENT BACK INTO SHAPE

## SHAPE

### Beating Addiction Through Yoga

Join me as we share a path from addiction to recovery
and a better future through Yoga

Esther Nagle
bentback@balanceandbreathe.co.uk

# Contents

# Foreword

When Esther asked me to write the foreword for her book I was overwhelmed with feelings; honoured to have been asked, excitement to be a part of her journey and humbled that she had asked me.

When Esther joined my first Yoga Teacher training course in April 2013, she brought with her a crazy ball of energy. If you could have drawn this energy, it would have been a massive fuzzy purple scribble! It had a manic, restless, unsettled feel about it albeit with a loud and vigorous friendliness. You could not miss her. She certainly would not melt into the background and was always clearly going to stand out in some way or other. Although on the face of it Esther, with this ball of wild unbalanced energy, was really not the likely candidate for a yoga teacher training course I was able to see past this and could see the earnest, eager, honest and respectful side of her.

The course is very intensive. It has to be in order for the individual to learn and change and take all of the teachings on so that yoga becomes a part of you and you become a part of yoga. None of Esther's changes would have been subtle, gentle changes as she went through her hugely transformative journey. She had a lot that needed to change. Although I have seen many people transform themselves and grow over the years, I have never seen anyone change in such a short time as much as Esther did. You see people change in Ananda Ashram, where I did my 6-month training, when they do that training. I believed that you could only get that kind of transformative change out there, but my first year of teacher training proved me wrong. Esther and her peers were all changing but Esther was to change at a rate of knots.

Every time Esther would turn up at the studio she would look different. Her face changed. Her complexion was healthier and had colour and the lines on her face lessened. Her eyes got brighter and her voice changed. Her physical body and her attitude softened and her energy completely changed. Her asthma and her general health both improved as did her diet and, as a consequence of all this, so did her lifestyle. Esther was changing who she wanted to spend her time with. She realised that she now liked her own company and could stay in on her own and not need distractions. By the end of the course Esther was a different person. Had you met the person she started out as and then met the Esther at the end of the course you would not have thought they were the same person at all! It was quite remarkable that someone could change that much and transform themselves for the better and hadn't done it in the ashram in India. Esther had done this huge transformation through hard work and dedication all by herself whilst living a busy life as a mum and a newly self-employed woman in Wales!

I won't say that it was easy for Esther as it wasn't. There were times when she didn't get up and do her practice and there were times when the homework was handed in late. There were a few tears and chats to talk things through that she battled with. There were probably times when she thought she couldn't do this anymore but something kept her going. While deep down most people fear the prospect of change, Esther wanted to change, she knew she had to change. This kept her going. She knew that she couldn't carry on as she had been and I believe her survival instinct had kicked in and she wanted to live...really live.

There is a saying that 'when the student is ready, the teacher will appear'. Google says it's a Buddhist zen saying but I know this though my yoga training in India. I strongly believe that this is the case with Esther. She was in the right place at the right time and doing the right thing. She was also conscious at the right time to recognise that. Had this consciousness not been there it may well have slipped her by. Had this been a different time or a different place then this overall effect would not have happened. Despite the darkness that she was in there must have been a light beckoning her and leading her to what would be her salvation. Her salvation was herself. Esther had been fortunate to find yoga and love yoga and trust in yoga for all of this to happen but it was all through the doing of herself. She did all the hard work and it paid off.

I'm so proud of Esther. I think the transformation that she has endured is amazing and I know that she is in such a good place to be able to help others who want to transform themselves as she has done. To teach from experience is the best place to teach from. You know what they are going through and where they are at, yet you know how to get to the place they want to get to. Esther has learnt so many amazing techniques and will be able to find those that are suitable for each situation. Not everyone will want to get onto a yoga mat and do a physical practice but there is so much more to it than that and Esther will be able to guide people in the right direction. She is very passionate about this and I believe she will go far and help many people along the way.

This book is a brutal but honest story of how life can tread you down and how you can get lost in that but it also tells the miraculous story of how you can be saved by saving yourself. With a little courage, persistence and the desire to survive at all costs this too is possible for anyone who knows that they need to change and wants for a better life. There are so many yogic lessons and guidelines that Esther has weaved into this book that I am astounded again by how much she has taken in and learnt without going to the ashram. If you are using this as a self-help book, then I recommend reading it more than once so that you can become aware of these lessons that clearly impacted on Esther in such a positive way. I strongly recommend contacting Esther if you have any questions on any of the content but whilst on your journey just remember these three things; don't judge yourself, don't compare yourself and don't beat yourself up.

**Om Ganapathiye Namah**

Yoga Chemmal Yogacharini Kalavathi Devi

Om Studio

# Gratitude

Gratitude is a vital aspect of a healthy life. It would therefore be remiss of me not to offer thanks to the people who have supported me in my journey through life, those who have helped me to get to the place where I can now write this book from a place of happiness.

Having looked back at my life in great detail over the last couple of years, I see that everything that happened to me, the 'good' and the 'bad', all contributed to me being in the place I am today. Without the 'bad' things in life, I would not have the stories to tell or be able share the lessons I have learned. I have learned so much more, and grown and deepened as a person more from the bad things than the good. So I would like to start by thanking the people who I have previously resented for the 'bad' things. While I am not going to name them, or go into details about their part in my story, they have played a significant part in the development of the being I am today, and without their input into my life, I, and my life would have been very different. It feels good to be able to thank people who have hurt me, but it has taken a long time, and a lot of inner work for me to be able to!

My deepest love and gratitude goes to the family and friends who have supported me and loved me despite me not always being deserving of that love. I have asked a lot of the people who care about me over the years, and have not always given much in return. I am eternally grateful for the many gifts they have given to me.

My deep, eternal and utterly unconditional love as always goes to my three wonderful sons. I have let them all down in the past through my actions, but at no point was my love for them in doubt. I am inordinately proud of who they all are, and take great delight in seeing them all grow into wonderful, loving, spirited, bright and honourable men. I hope that I can be a good role model to them now that I am living my life with more dignity than I used to, and that they can continue to forgive my mistakes of the past.

While I am grateful to all the Yoga teachers I have learned from over the years, I can never express my thanks and deep gratitude enough to Kalavathi Devi of Om Studio, Cardiff. When I arrived at her studio in April 2014, I was a mess of stress, ego and tension. I asked a lot of Kalavathi in the early months of our relationship, and she has always given me so much, given me opportunities, friendship, love and compassion. I am deeply honoured to have been lucky enough to meet, and be taught by her, and am proud to call her 'teacher'. Through her training, I was introduced to the magnificent teachings of Swami Gitananda, his wife Ammaji, and his son Dr Ananda Balayogi Bhavanani, and Ananda Ashram. I am truly blessed to have had these teachings in my life. To say that the course I engaged in was life changing would be understating the case considerably – it saved me, of that I have no doubt. The life I live now that I have Gitananda Yoga in my life, and the life I will continue to live, with these teachings guiding me every step of the way, is a life filled with joy, fulfilment and happiness that I could only dream of before. I am constantly

# Introduction

Yoga offers many tools that can help you to take control of your life and break free of stress and addictions. Through this book I will share with you some of these tools. My understanding of these tools deepens every time I read or think about them. I am not claiming that this is an 'expert' book. I have only been aware of most of these tools for less than two years, I am far from expert. I simply wish to share with you how my life has been enriched and maybe even saved by the teachings of some very wise people and how these teachings could help you develop your own toolkit for life. There is much I would like to explore deeper, particularly in relation to the neuroscience of addiction, recovery and Yoga, but I simply do not have a sufficient in depth understanding of the science nor am I likely to have in the near future. At another time of my life, I would like to study this in further detail but this is not an option now.

For about 20 years I used alcohol, cigarettes and recreational drugs, as well as a whole host of other addictive behaviours, to hide my deep seated unhappiness from the world and from myself. Terrified of facing my emotions head on, I was unable to sleep sober because of the constant negative self-talk from an inner critic that seemed to loathe me completely. I turned to alcohol and other harmful behaviours to give me a feeling of escape and relief from the self-loathing. I longed for a feeling of 'normality' to enable me to put on a front of happiness and confidence that were non-existent in me sober.

In reality of course, these behaviours simply fuelled the self-loathing and shame that brought me to them in the first place. Going to work with a hangover, feeling dreadful and knowing I probably look awful, and smell as bad didn't add to my self-esteem.

Following a breakdown in 2013, I found myself in Yoga teacher training, something I had wanted to do for many years. I was amazed to learn that there are depths to Yoga I had never even known about. As I learned about the many layers and threads there are in Yoga, I began to see that what I was actually discovering was a way I could live that may actually bring some peace and clarity to my life. I realised it could bring me far greater health and vitality than I had ever imagined possible and could set me free from much of the unhappiness I had lived with for so many years.

As I learned to breathe properly, to relax and to release tension in my body, I also learned to look at my behaviour, my thoughts, my actions, and to look at how I was living. I was forced to ask myself if I was I living in a way that was ever going to bring me inner peace. I most certainly hadn't been. Gradually through my practice and contemplation of these concepts and with a desire to change my behaviour I began to feel lighter, more at peace and happier. I was able to find acceptance of the demons that had blighted my life, to forgive myself and others for hurt I had experienced in the past. I saw that I could create a better future not by dwelling in the past, but by accepting, forgiving and learning lessons.

In this book I will share some carefully selected stories of my own journey, I will also be including some blog posts I had written on my website, posts that I have had good feedback for and that have helped people. There will be practices you can incorporate into your own life, and invitations to contemplate your life in a gentle but deep way. It is my sincere hope that you will find something of value in these pages that can help you find some balance in your life whether you are dealing with addiction or not. We all, to some extent, find a way to soothe ourselves against the world, the tools Yoga offers us can benefit us all.

# The Long and Wine Filled Road

When I discovered, at the age of 16, that alcohol gave me a mask behind which to hide my insecurities and low self-esteem, I felt as though a great gift had been given to me. I drank only at weekends, and generally had a good time. I was able to talk to people, to relax, to dance, and even more amazingly, I was able to talk to boys I was attracted to. This alone, to a girl so insecure that she was completely incapable of talking to boys sober, made alcohol seem like nothing short of a miracle potion!

When I was 20, my life fell apart in ways I could never have imagined possible, and the low self-esteem developed into deep self-loathing and a conviction that I was a despicable person. The mask became a comfort blanket to soothe my deep pain and I turned more and more to alcohol, and other drugs to escape the inner critic who constantly wanted to tell me how awful I was.

This established a pattern of coping strategies that developed into total dependence on alcohol within a short space of time, a dependence that raged for over 20 years (punctuated only by pregnancy and breast feeding related abstinence), accompanied by increasingly poor mental health. As my addiction deepened, I lost countless hours of my life. I got so used to the blackouts that I began to think it was normal to forget huge chunks of the previous day. I experienced 'the shakes' more times than I ever wanted to count and would find myself craving alcohol, tasting it in my mind so clearly I would have to have it. I would construct any excuse possible to drink

# The Yoga Path, the path to recovery

This healing led me to my Yoga teacher, to the Om Studio and to Gitananda Yoga, and the most incredible year of learning, releasing, forgiving and healing. I had gone to Yoga classes for several years before this point and it had definitely made me feel better while I was in the class, but the effects always seemed short lived. I would go home and open a bottle of wine, roll a joint and smoke some cigarettes. I never learned how to relax, never really saw Yoga as anything other than a way to improve my body shape and get a little bit of time out from my life.

Through the training I received from Kalavathi at the Om Studio, I leaned about the teachings of Swami Gitananda, of Rishiculture Ashtanga Yoga (Gitananda Yoga) and the teachings of Maharishi Patanjali in the Yoga Sutras.

I have often joked that I experienced about 5 years' worth of therapy in the space of that year. This may not be such a joke. I have had counselling in the past; while the counsellors I saw were very good, I never experienced the massive shifts that I got during my year in the Om Studio.

That the course changed my life is understating the fact; I would go so far as to say it *saved* my life. On October 12 2014, after just 7 months of learning, intensive personal development work and physical practices that were changing me at every level of my being, I woke up one morning with the hangover from hell and decided I was not going to do this to myself anymore. I didn't declare I was quitting drinking at that point; having had some clear insights into my self-sabotaging tendencies, I knew myself well enough to know that even at 41 I would rebel and kick back against any attempt to control my behaviour, even when (*especially* when), I was the one doing the controlling. I simply went through a few weeks of 'not drinking today' and when I attended my brother's wedding and shunned the free flowing, expensive red wine in favour of delicious, refreshing, non-alcoholic fizzy elderflower cordial, I knew I had turned a corner. I could have drunk that night, no one would have minded or tried to stop me, but my experience of the day and evening would have been very different indeed.

From that night on I knew I was no longer a drinker, no longer an alcoholic. I had barely begun to use the word about myself when I started referring to it in the past tense. I choose not to identify myself as an alcoholic in recovery, or such similar terms, because I am such a different person now.

The practices I learned during those first 7 months of teacher training shifted things in my mind. I released a lot of the physical tension I had carried around with me for years. I learned to breathe and gained all the numerous benefits of that, I learned to still my mind a little, to let thoughts pass and to change my reactions to challenges. I was able to sleep well, a new experience completely as I had not slept well since I was a child, scared of the murderers that were obviously going to come to attack us at night. Even though I had stopped being afraid of imaginary intruders, the anxieties just evolved. Yoga helped me see that I no longer needed to live in fear.

necessary. Yoga gave me a new way to be, a new Me to be, the Me that I had always dreamed of being, the Me I had referred to as 'Fantasy Esther' for several years.

The ultimate aim of Yoga is freedom; it helps us find our true self, the one we hide behind our masks; addiction was my mask. I have felt more in tune with the real me since giving up drinking than I ever did when I was drinking. The alcoholic wasn't the real me, so why would I want to keep referring to myself as an alcoholic?

I have often wondered if I swapped my dependency on alcohol for a dependency on Yoga. I am fairly sure that if I went a month without any form of yoga practice in my life I would again become at risk of addiction as I would lose touch with my coping techniques and lose connection to the real me. I am not prepared to ever find out. So yes, I now have a dependency on yoga, I have a yoga habit, but isn't our whole life largely a series of habits? Some are good for us, some are destructive. Better to have one good habit than 20 destructive ones.

# What is yoga?

If I was to ask you what you think Yoga is, you would probably think about a slow paced form of exercise, of people tying themselves in knots and sitting cross legged chanting 'Om'. You may have some ideas of the type of people who 'do' Yoga – hippies, dropouts, very thin, flexible people and 'yummy mummies' to name a few stereotypes. You may think Yoga is linked to a religion, probably Hinduism or possibly Buddhism.

Yoga is many things. Yoga can be seen, as it is by many, as an exercise system that you 'do' once or twice a week by attending a class. If you regularly practice the postures, breath exercises and relaxations you will benefit immensely. Just one Yoga class can offer a huge range of benefits to body and mind. However, simply doing this excludes you from the many other benefits that are to be gained from integrating Yoga into your life on a deeper level.

According to the Yoga Sutras, one of the key scriptures of Yoga, it is 'the cessation of the whirlpools of the subconscious mind'. It is a way to achieve peace and calm, to bring the subconscious mind to our awareness, learn to control it, and discover the True Self that can be found once these whirlpools have stopped.

Swami Gitananda tells us that Yoga is "a way of integrating your whole nature, so that all aspects of your life work in harmony, one with another". This is the true meaning of Yoga. Yoga comes from the Sanskrit word 'Yuj', which means to 'yoke' or to 'join as one'. Its traditional primary purpose is to bring us closer to the Divine. While some may see this as 'God', to the ancient Yogis, we are all Divine, Yoga is the way we connect with the Divine aspect of ourselves, our eternal soul. Yoga is a truly holistic practice. It connects mind, body and soul together. It is so much more than an exercise class.

Many people link Yoga with Pilates. Now, while there are some similarities in the postures used in Pilates, as it borrows very heavily from Yoga, Pilates is entirely body focussed. Its purpose is to create very strong muscles and to develop good control. This is, of course, a very good thing, we need strong muscles and good muscle control. I used to go to Pilates classes years ago, and loved it – it is a very effective form of exercise. I was also doing a 20-minute physical Yoga practice most days, and created the best physique I have ever had through this regime. But Pilates is only about the body, it is not a holistic practice the way Yoga is.

Yoga has a deeply spiritual element to it, but it is not a religion, nor is it connected to a religion. It grew out of Hinduism, but it was a radical departure from its constraints. Yoga does not require religious faith, but if you have a belief, it will deepen it. Swami Gitananda tells us that Yoga will make you be better at whatever you are, better Christian, better Hindu, better Muslim, better human. Yoga is a way to connect to our own personal Spirituality. There is a world of difference between religion and spirituality. Spirituality is "simply the discovery of our authentic self without any trimmings or labels which gives us a rich source of values and a deeper meaning to life, whatever our religion". (Ed and Deb Shapiro, Huffington Post, 2011)

Like Hinduism, Yoga teaches us that we are not our body or our mind, but that we are an eternal soul that lives through many different lifetimes in order to learn lessons, grow and evolve. It teaches us that our soul moves through various life forms, getting closer to human at every step and once we find ourselves in a human life form we continue to evolve towards the Divine, to Samadhi, or Freedom. This freedom from the cycle of rebirth is the ultimate aim of the soul.

The Yogic way of thinking tells us that we are born into the life we are in now because this life is going to teach us lessons that are vital to the evolution of our soul. While this is a hard concept to grasp, and not one that will work for everyone, it is one that I personally find very comforting. It gives meaning to our suffering. To know that we can choose to see the pain or the lesson is empowering. If we are able to see the lessons, then not only will our life be happier but we will aid the evolution of our soul.

# Yoga Sutras

Rishiculture Ashtanga Yoga, the tradition of Yoga I was trained in, is based entirely on the Yoga Sutras. Codified by Maharishi Patanjali, who, it is believed, lived around 1500BC, they represent the first written record of teachings that had been passed down orally from Guru to Student for possibly thousands of years prior to this. They are a series of short sutras, or verses, which, though short, contain enough meaning to warrant essays, dissertations, entire books and probably entire careers to understand fully. Maharishi Patanjali was a very wise man who is believed to have also written about Ayurveda, the ancient Indian medicine system and grammar.

In the 195 (or 196, depending on the interpretation you are working from) Sutras of this epic work, Patanjali lays down the problems with the human condition, and offers us solutions and the path to happiness and Enlightenment. This path is Yoga. If we can gain this peace in our mind, then we can learn the True Self that we really are, see through the mask of who we think we are, and find peace and connection to the world, our Self and the Higher Self (who or whatever you call God).

Patanjali tells us that the general human condition is one of unhappiness and that we seek happiness in the external conditions of life. We can never be content though until we realise that happiness only exists within. Thankfully, to those who wish to find it, Patanjali offers, through the Yoga Sutras, a guide to help us.

The Yoga Sutras are a clear insight into the human condition, which, if accompanied by the guidance of a knowledgeable and experienced teacher, can provide us with great insights about our individual selves and our society. Swami Gitananda's Step by Step course provided the groundwork for my own understanding of this great work and this is being further deepened by Dr Ananda Balayogi Bhavanani's 'Understanding the Yoga Darshan'.

In the Yoga Sutras, Patanjali sets out the path to freedom and enlightenment through Yoga. These are the 'Eight Limbs of Yoga' and are the basis of the system of Yoga known as Rishiculture Ashtanga Yoga, or Gitananda Yoga, that I have trained in.

Mind, body and soul are intrinsically linked. We cannot have a healthy mind with an unhealthy body, and an unhealthy mind leads to an unhealthy body and soul. Patanjali's Eight Limbs tell us the steps we can take to ensure that all aspects of our being are well nourished and are working at their full potential.

The Eight Limbs of Yoga are: -

**Yama** – these are about curbing the base animal instincts in us. They are concerned with how we behave in the physical world

**Niyama** – these are to do with elevating us to a higher human life, to raise us above the animal and evolve our consciousness so that we can become the best humans we can be.

**Asana** – this is the physical postures that we in the West often think of as 'Yoga'. They are a small but important aspect of a wider Yoga life. Asanas exist to enable us to train the body to be able to sit for long periods of time to practice Pranayama

**Pranayama** – this is control of the breath to enable control of the mind, and maximum intake of Prana, the Universal Energy, and oxygen into the body.

**Pratyahara** - this can come about through the previous 4 steps, and particularly through Pranayama. It is said to be the moment when Yoga practice moves from the external to the internal. It is the control of the senses by cultivating and perfecting them. This is the activity that many people know of as meditation.

**Dharana** – this cannot be achieved until we have mastered Pratyahara. Dharana is the process of controlling the mind to concentrate and focus, and to ignore the sensory information from outside. It is the development of awareness of the activity of the mind, but not a surrender to it. It is developing awareness of the power of the mind to transcend this activity and actually control the emotions and sensory reactions

**Dhyana** – once Dharana has been perfected, we can then slip effortlessly into Dhyana, the state of meditation in its true form. Dharana is concentration on an object or thought for a short period of time, Dhyana is when the concentration is held for an extended time. Dhyana, or true meditation, is a state we achieve through total dedication and skilful control of our mind and senses, and is not something we can simply 'do'.

**Samadhi** - Samadhi is Cosmic Consciousness, the final stage in the Soul's evolutionary journey, and the 8th Limb of Yoga as described by Patanjali. Samadhi is 'Awareness of Awareness'. When one achieves Samadhi, the mind and self, stop focusing on the individual, the ego, the 'I', and become part of the Universe. Samadhi is what we would term enlightenment, and what Hindus and Yogis believe is the arrival of the soul at its ultimate destination, freedom from the reincarnation cycle, the soul becomes one with the Divine. Samadhi comes in stages, and has many elements to it, some of which last for ever, and some which are short lived. The early stages of Samadhi, which can be the shorter lasting phases, are known as Sabikalpa Samadhi, while Nirbikalpa Samadhi is a deeper state of being. When Samadhi is attained and perfected in the Nirbikalpa state, the soul or Jiva is known as a Jivan Mukhta, a free, realised soul and is freed from the cycle of birth and death.

The first four limbs of Yoga – Yama, Niyama, Asana and Pranayama, are called the Outer Limbs, and are the very bedrock of the higher spiritual practices. The Outer limbs are very practical and physical. They are concerned with the physical body, our involvement with society and the evolution of the individual towards the higher spiritual plane. These four outer limbs are the Bahiranga, also known as Hatha Yoga. By consciously applying these four lower limbs to your life you will naturally create a stress free, healthy, content life. These must be very strong and secure before the next 4 limbs can begin to be built.

The subsequent four limbs are Pratyahara, Dharana. Dhyana and Samadhi. They are known as the Inner Limbs. Collectively these are Antaranga. The Antaranga are totally dependent on the firm foundation of the Bahiranga; without this firm grounding the seeker will not be successful in attaining the Inner Limbs. As this book is about my journey to resilience and recovery, I will not be delving deeply into these limbs, as I have yet to achieve them. It is the Outer Limbs; the Bahiranga, that are the limbs that helped me to free myself from addiction.

While the true aim of this path is spiritual enlightenment, it offers all the tools needed to develop resilience and coping strategies that will enable us to move from unhappiness, suffering, stress and addiction to find emotional and physical freedom; after all, spiritual freedom is not possible when we are in the grip of an addiction that consumes us.

In the Sutras, Patanjali makes many interesting observations on the nature of human suffering that are as relevant now as they were over 2000 years ago. It seems that humans haven't really learned much over the millennia; maybe we just found new ways to inflict suffering on ourselves!

# The Eightfold Path

The path of Yoga, the Yoga Marga requires certain behaviours from anyone who tries to walk it. You cannot achieve spiritual freedom (Samadhi) through 'meditation' alone, it requires behaviour changes, attitude changes, lifestyle changes. The same is true of recovery. Sobriety is more than the absence of the substance of addiction, there is a whole mindset, behaviour and lifestyle change that needs to accompany that absence. As well as requiring these changes, Yoga and recovery help us to make these changes. As we develop greater resilience through the practices of Yoga, we realise that life is easier, healthier, less stressful, and we are more whole as people. This makes a life free of stress, unhappiness and addiction far more possible.

The Buddha, who lived many years after Patanjali wrote the Yoga Sutras, taught about The Eightfold Path. This is made up of the Eight Noble Concepts that the Buddha said were crucial to achieving spiritual enlightenment. They are also very valuable concepts to keep in mind during recovery.

The elements of the Eightfold path in relation to addiction and spiritual enlightenment are:

*Correct understanding*

We must understand that our view of the world is affected by our senses and perceptions and endeavour to see past this to see the world as it really is. We don't experience the world as it is, we experience the world the way our mind is conditioned to see it. We see things relative to our past experiences, our likes and dislikes, our unique, individual perception of the world. We must develop awareness of the power of the mind to influence how we see the world, and to appreciate that what we think is real is not really so. For example, we might think that we 'need' a drink to help us deal with a stressful situation but this craving has actually been created by the patterns in our mind telling us that stressful situation can be solved with a drink. This construct of our mind can be sidestepped and we can move past the craving. It is not always easy, I am not going to pretend it is, but with the tools provided by Yoga it is possible.

*Correct Aims*

We must ensure that our motives for action and our behaviour are pure; this will help us on our Yoga Marga. We must ensure that we harm no one through our actions. Sometimes though, doing the right thing for our spiritual evolution means that we hurt other people's feelings. For example, your self-study may make you realise that a relationship no longer serves you, maybe you are with someone who is still using and is not sympathetic to your desire to quit. In this situation, we would be right to end the relationship, but we should do it in a kind and respectful way, with gratitude for the friendship that served us at the time. Recovery from addiction may shine a light on how self focussed your behaviour has been throughout your addiction. This is normal, addiction does make us self centred, or addiction centred, as the addiction makes us behave in ways we wouldn't otherwise, and we might feel guilt and shame that we have let others down. Instead of focussing on the negative feelings, look at how you can make amends and look to put things right with your behaviour from now on.

*Correct use of speech*

We need to bear in mind that our words have impact and we should not use them lightly. Always think before you speak and consider the likely impact of what you say. Do not engage in frivolous or harmful speech. We should ensure that we don't cause harm to ourselves or others with our words and don't use our words to gossip and spread misinformation. This correct use of speech is very important to bear in mind when thinking of how you speak to yourself. We are often our own worst enemies; we speak to ourselves in ways that we would never consider speaking to others. So be aware of this, and ensure that you are speaking well to yourself as well as others. Try to notice your self talk, and don't allow the negative thoughts to dominate any longer.

*Correct conduct*

We must make sure that our actions at all times reflect the higher path we are on; we must ensure that we avoid conflict where the actions are low while the mind is high as this will create a duality what will impede growth. For example, if you are trying to give up drinking, spending your days in a pub is probably not the most helpful action to take. Focussing on long term goals rather than short term effects will be a good way to ensure that our actions are inspired by the higher aspirations rather than to spontaneously act in the moment. Be on the guard for triggers, and practice breath control so that when situations that might test your sobriety arise, you can take those valuable deep breaths to calm you before you respond.

*Correct Mode of Livelihood*

It is important that the way we earn a living is in keeping with our goals, or at least not in direct conflict with them. The spiritual aspirant should aim to work in a role in which they are able to help others and work for the greater good. So too should the person on the path to recovery. It would do me no good, for example either spiritually or in terms of ensuring my own recovery, to go and work in a pub, it would be totally at odds with my own interests and my desire to help others move away from dependence on alcohol.

*Correct effort*

If we are serious about recovery or spiritual growth, then we need to give full and committed effort to that journey. Half-hearted efforts bring half the results and will leave us feeling unsatisfied. Swami Gitananda tells us that any effort we make is rewarded, but if we are serious about making significant changes, we must commit to creating new habits and practising them daily. Ammaji, Swami Gitananda's wife, teaches the maxim of the 3R's – Repetition, Regularity and Rhythm as being vital to the yoga life, they also apply to a life of recovery.

*Correct intellectual activity*

The relentless pursuit of satisfying an addiction does not give the mind chance to develop and grow. Give the brain new opportunities to expand through meditation and inner life study. Bringing Yogic ways into life will make this higher focus of the mind easy as Yoga lends itself well to higher intellectual activity.

*Correct Contemplation*

The mind should be kept at a level where intuition and insight can be developed. Don't allow too many distractions to reach the senses and learn to minimise the impact of the distractions that do present themselves.

Anyone who can truly and wholeheartedly walk the Eightfold Path will find their way to enlightenment and inner freedom. This same path can guide us towards resilience, and away from addiction. It is not an easy path to tread though; there are many barriers to our progress along the way. Pantanjali tells us that these barriers all stem from Avidya; ignorance of our True Self. If we can cultivate real awareness of the universal, eternal nature of our true self we will be able to walk the path with ease.

# Just say No?

As a child growing up in the 1980s, I was exposed to, and very emotionally affected by, the Just Say No campaign by the Thatcher government.

Zammo, the Grange Hill character who succumbed to heroin addiction, was a favourite of mine and I hated seeing him suffer. The images and language that national anti-heroin campaign used terrified me and left me with the impression that all 'drugs' meant a life of pain, misery, isolation and early death. I became so passionate about the subject I even wrote to the office of Mrs T, imploring her to never legalise cannabis (how I disagree with that teenage ideal now).

The overall message I got from this campaign was 'All drugs are bad, all drug addicts are untrustworthy and dishonest and if you so much as look at heroin, you WILL be hooked and you WILL die a horrible death. The only defence against addiction is 'Just say NO!'

Fast forward to my late teenage years, I left my Rhondda home in 1993 shrouded in despair, self-loathing, abject misery and a certainty that I was a truly despicable person. I was already showing clear signs of depression and alcohol dependence, although I didn't recognise it at the time. I had been a smoker for 5 years, had a penchant for recreational drugs such as speed and acid and a regular marijuana habit. I didn't go far, my efforts to try to improve my life by getting A Levels and aiming for university took me about 10 miles away, to a bedsit inhabited by drinkers, smokers, drug users and addicts. It was only ever meant to be temporary but I ended up staying there for 18 months. During this time, I found myself sinking deeper and deeper into addiction and self-loathing. I only managed to get one A Level, and didn't make it to university, but that wasn't because of the drugs (not directly anyway), I was offered a job and wanted money more than I wanted an education.

Around this time, a new drug seemed to be making its way around the valley. Heroin use seemed to be on the rise. I remember hearing reports of men around my age dying from the substance. I have always felt very grateful that I was not in the Rhondda much at this time — I always felt that if I had been in proximity to heroin that I would have tried it and become addicted. I thought this was because heroin was "really addictive', that the substance would somehow hook into my brain at the first try and never let me go again.

I was partly right in this assessment. If I had tried heroin in those days, I would have almost certainly become addicted to it. I was wrong though in my concept of why. If the substance itself was so addictive, patients would leave hospital post-surgery addicted to morphine. If addiction was purely substance based there would be no such thing as shopping addiction, gambling addiction, social media addiction. If addiction was just about the substance everyone who ever drunk alcohol would be an alcoholic.

My risk of addiction wasn't about the heroin I might have taken but because the heroin would have soothed something in me that desperately needed soothing, just as the alcohol I was consuming in increasing quantities was doing. I was an emotional and psychological mess; I was consumed with regret, shame and despair at the direction my life was taking. I sought oblivion and a way to pretend to be happy every way I could. Heroin would have definitely offered me that.

I was drinking to the point of passing out and total memory loss, smoking pot till I couldn't speak. I loved the fake highs that acid gave me until the psychedelic trips would freak me out. I would sleep with any man that showed the slightest interest in me (because if they wanted to sleep with me it meant they liked me, or at least found me attractive, didn't it?) I certainly couldn't understand how people could go out and have just one or two drinks. A night out when I didn't receive any male attention would fuel my conviction that I was ugly and worthless, but the times when I did get attention it would still feel hollow, and I would still come away feeling ugly and worthless.

None of this oblivion seeking brought me happiness, fulfilment or any respite. It only made it worse. Day to day reality was filled with the voice in my head telling me I was worthless and the activities I became addicted to quietened that noise for a while, although sometimes it would make it just shout louder. The morning after was always accompanied by a sense of shame, a foggy head and often a desire to get away from the nameless naked body next to me. The voice would tell me that I was now even more disgusting because of what I had done the night before. The cycle continued.

None of this was to do with the substances themselves. If I could have found oblivion in a packet of salt and vinegar crisps, I would have done. Addictions arise from a need for something to be pacified. The addiction is merely the vehicle by which people find this calm. As Gabor Mate says in 'In the Realm of Hungry Ghosts',

*'Addiction has biological, chemical, neurobiological, psychological, medical, emotional, social, political, economic and spiritual underpinnings, and perhaps others I haven't mentioned.'*

Addiction is not something we can simply say no to. While it is true that we can choose not to indulge in the behaviour in the first place, we cannot know that we will become addicted until it is too late. By the point we realise that we are addicted, significant changes have happened in the brain that means we cannot just say no. We can't simply decide not to drink, to smoke, to inject, to click on the Facebook link, to go shopping or to seduce the next partner. The addiction fills a deep need in us and that need creates chemical changes in the brain; we cannot beat this without tacking the underlying issues, and developing resilience skills to enable us to cope without our addiction.

Dr Mate describes addiction as being,

*'Any repeated behaviour, substance related or not, in which a person feels compelled to persist, regardless of its negative impact on his life or the life of others.'*

There is a real agony in the mind of the addict around the addiction – a real battle between pleasure and pain. The addiction numbs against pain, fills the void and offers a brief taste of pleasure and fulfilment. This quickly evaporates though and becomes a need that creates pain and suffering again. This constant lurching between pleasure and pain, with oblivion, emotional release, suffering and craving in between is not a lifestyle choice any one would aspire to.

Alcoholics Anonymous tells its members that they will forever be alcoholics, that they will never be free and that they must forever bind themselves to the fellowship and to their addiction. From a neuroscience point of view, this is correct; addiction is a chronic, incurable disease of the brain that damages and destroys neural pathways. However, new neural pathways can be created through the development of new habits and new ways of thinking. It is possible to create a new version of life in which we fully acknowledge the past, and the very real risks that lie in relapse, but don't cling to the identification of 'alcoholic'.

A Yogic approach to this will tell us that by continuing to identify with the addiction to such an extent, we are keeping ourselves bound to the suffering that accompanies the addiction. It keeps us focussing on what we don't have, what we have given up, rather than on moving forward. We should look at where we are *right* now, accept that our past has lead us here, but move forward into a future that is created from the present moment. I can't ever risk drinking again, but I gleefully tell people I *used to be an alcoholic*; I don't wish to continue to label myself this way.

I am no longer identified by an addiction.

I am no longer an alcoholic.

# Will the real Esther Nagle please stand up?

The struggle to find an identity that I am happy with has been at the heart of every problem in my life. Yoga helps us to get to the root of who we are, it helps us to look beyond the human dimension of ourselves and get to know our spiritual, divine essence.

Before we can do this we do need to have an understanding of ourselves in this physical form and how we have come to be the person we see in the mirror today.

The Wikipedia page on identity tells us this about identity:

"In psychology, sociology, anthropology and philosophy, identity is the conception, qualities, beliefs, and expressions that make a person (self-identity) ... different from others."

The page is very long and covers lots of information about theoretical ideas on the subject; our identity is a complicated construct that is ever evolving, even when we might think it has remained unchanged. The insights I share here have been achieved through Swadhyaya which will be discussed in more detail in the chapter on the Niyamas.

One of my earliest memories of how my identity defined me is associated with my name. Being called Esther and having buck teeth was not a great combination in the decade that brought us Esther Rantzen and 'That's Life!' I remember being surrounded by children in the playground all chanting 'sausages' at me. I was baffled as I didn't know anything about the 'talking dog' that had appeared on the show and as a 4-year-old child, I just felt frightened. For many years I was haunted by this woman, despite not even watching her on TV. As a teenager I was relieved to get a brace to correct the teeth that had caused me such grief but of course, a mouthful of metal for 18 months became a new source of entertainment for my peers and something else for me to feel insecure about.

I grew up feeling very different, and struggled for many years to work out who I am. The identity I created for myself was not a healthy one, and was created out of the very negative image I had of myself. Patterns of self-destructive, self-sabotaging behaviour were created in my teens, and began to shape how I saw myself and how I presented myself to the world. When I made catastrophic decisions that changed the course of my life forever, my negative view of myself was confirmed, and the self-sabotage was taken to new heights. As far as I could see, I was a terrible person so deserved nothing but misery. This created a vicious cycle of negative emotions fuelling the self-destructive habits, which added to the negative emotions. I remember on several occasions when I was 'Esther the drunken mess' thinking 'but this isn't who I am supposed to be', feeling that there was someone else living my life for me and that somewhere along the line I had accidentally fallen into the wrong life.

It was quite a shock, but a liberating one, to know that the reason I hadn't achieved my goals in life due to this established pattern of self-sabotage. A hard lesson to learn, but if I have been responsible for every failure, I can be responsible for every success.

During the last few years of my unhappiness, another version of me existed in my mind; I called her 'fantasy Esther'. She was happy, she was healthy, she lived in a tidy house, and she had happy children who she could play with for hours. She didn't have an internet connected device in her hand constantly, she didn't smoke and she didn't drink. She lived a simple, joyful life of nature, love and peace. I envied her so much, and desperately wanted to be her. After a few months of yoga training I realised that 'she' was me living according to the ideals of Yoga.

This realisation has been one of the many gifts that my yoga training has given me. The goal of Yoga is to help us to connect with our true and divine self. Before we can do this we have to connect deeply to and understand the person we are have been. We have to learn to accept who we are, to forgive the mistakes of the past and to identify the parts of us that could work better. We have to take steps to become the very best person we can be. This enables us to be 'fit' for spiritual enlightenment.

Very recently, I have realised that I need to stop looking towards 'Fantasy Esther' as someone to aspire to be and start to accept that I am her already. I need to be her in the present moment and stop holding her up as a future ideal; a fantasy.

Learning to accept and forgive past Esther has not always been easy; there has been a catalogue of 'mistakes' to process. Most of these experiences are not for this book, but the process of writing has led me to write extensively about the past in great detail. This writing is safely hidden away in my laptop and notebooks, not for anyone else to read, but writing it helped me to heal a great deal of wounds.

I no longer look at my 'failings' as mistakes or evidence of a wasted life. Yes, there are times in my life when I could have applied myself, been more focussed or made different choices. Looking back now though, I wonder if that really is the case. I could have done things differently, what would I be now?

The person I am today as I sit and write these words is the product of every 'mistake', every squandered opportunity and every episode of poor judgement.

I made the choices in the past because of who I was then, and they have created the present me, who is now able to look back and learn and is determined to move forward making better choices each time. I like the present me, so how can I regret any of those mistakes?

Much of our unhappiness in life comes from either worrying about the past or the future. We can't change the past, we can only learn from it. Worrying about the future doesn't do anything to change it; it only causes us anxiety. The only way to create the future we want is to live right now in the present moment.

The easiest way to do this is through the breath, I will share more with you about this in the chapter on Pranayama. Happiness is, I think, that feeling you get when you are comfortable in your own skin. You can be comfortable in that skin whatever else is going on around you. Life still throws rocks at me sometimes, and I do get stressed and upset but I still manage to retain that sense of who I am. I know that I am ok and I am up to the challenge of whatever comes my way.

I recently met a woman who reminded me of who I used to be. It unnerved me a lot. It was very unexpected, and I found it very stressful. It caused me to examine myself again in some detail. I took great lessons from this experience and it focused my mind on the importance of maintain Yoga in my life.

I stand before you now as a woman who is still not entirely fully connected with the true Esther but as someone who is on a very enjoyable journey to find her. Every experience I have, every book I read, every person I meet teaches me something. Every day I learn something new about myself and how I interact with the world. Sometimes this leads me to revelations that make me feel happy, sometimes the realisations I have cause me pain, but I embrace each and every one as a gift and an opportunity to grow a little more.

We are constantly changing and evolving, our cells are constantly renewing, every breath is an invitation to release and let go of the past. If you are aware of aspects of yourself that you don't like, if you are holding you back from being the person you know you can be, then Yoga can help you uncover your truth.

# Are you there God, it's me, Esther

I remember my first spiritual feeling as an adult. I was pregnant and on a short holiday in the Gower with Liam's father, we argued and I had walked away in a rage. Unable to drown my sorrows in the pub I passed, I went and sat by the sea. I watched and listened as the tide lapped against the shore. The peace of this and the eternal quality of the movement of the sea really struck me, I remember being very calmed by the notion that, in the greater scheme of things petty human quarrels pale into insignificance. The sea would carry on hitting the shore regardless of what we did. Being in the presence of this far greater, everlasting thing and this feeling of insignificance comforted me completely. I returned to him considerably calmed, but never forgot that moment. At the time though, I failed to recognise it as a spiritual encounter, but I think that really, it is the definition of spirituality – that sense of being part something far bigger, of connection, and finding inner peace within that connection seems to me to be what spirituality is.

I don't think it is any coincidence that I had this sense of connection when I was not drinking. By this point in my life, I was already pretty heavily alcohol dependent and had been for several years but was taking a break during my pregnancy. I have come to understand addiction as a spiritual issue and as I have progressed in my recovery I recognise that how spiritually disconnected I used to be.

I grew up going to church and being immersed in the stories and legends of Christianity. I didn't enjoy going to church, because it was cold and the services seemed to go on forever, but I did enjoy the faith. I was confirmed when I was 11, but sometime after that I was pondering the concept of man being made in God's image. This was perplexing to me as I could only imagine that this meant that God was like us, in a human body. In true childish naïveté, I asked the Rector why, if this was the case, God didn't fall out of heaven, as a human body must surely be subject to gravity. He told me he didn't know. What I now suspect is that he didn't have time to answer my question, but in that moment I was floored. I almost felt my faith disintegrating before my eyes. If the Rector didn't know the answer to that most basic question about the nature of God, how could I trust him on anything else? As soon as I was allowed I stopped going to church. Since then, I have only attended for weddings and funerals. There has been the odd occasion when I have felt compelled to go out of seeking something indescribable, but I have been uncomfortable saying most of the words in the services.

In my late teens, my childhood love of the Beatles morphed into absolute devotion, obsession and a real feeling that I was living in the wrong era. I discovered, through my love of George Harrison in particular, the religions of the East. I was very drawn to the mystical qualities of Harrison's lyrics, of the Indian instruments he used in his work and the sense of contentment he seemed to radiate, especially in his songs where he talked about his love of God. I felt far more comfortable with the concept of reincarnation than with the idea that this life is all there is. The idea that you get one chance to get it right before your eternal fate is sealed to either in eternal Heaven or

Hell didn't sit well with me. I was fascinated by Hare Krishna devotees. I loved seeing them in Swansea when I lived there, they always seemed so happy, so utterly delighted with their lot. I loved the orange robes, the music and the chanting. Oddly though, whenever I thought about pursuing my interest in these other faiths, my fear of other people's ideas would haunt me, and I would think 'but I'm supposed to be a Christian, if I am going to be religious it has to be in a church or how could I tell the family?' I never did anything about it.

When I did my Primary teacher training, one of my favourite subjects was Religious Education. I loved learning about the religions, and seeing the similarities between them. There are so many. At their core the message about how we should live on this world together is the same; be good to each other, take care of your body and respect whatever force you believe created the world.

In the meantime, of course, I was working hard on my addictions and depression. Descending deeper into alcohol and marijuana dependence, these were my sources of happiness and contentment. My gods were drugs, alcohol and music, and oh, how I worshiped them.

When my brother, who had planned to train to be an Anglican Priest, died, I found myself raging at a God I didn't even believe in. As well as being utterly distraught at his death, I was furious at the fact that he had believed it all and had wanted to 'do God's work', and yet he died at 30, when I, the heathen with no belief system other than 'a drink and a spliff will solve it' was seemingly ok. It seemed that any hope of me ever 'getting' religion was over.

I had been going to Yoga classes with various teachers for a long time before I had the breakdown that eventually guided me to Yoga teacher training. Despite knowing intellectually that Yoga was related to spirituality, I had never really had any experience of that; I had always really understood Yoga as being about the body, not the soul.

The understanding I gained of Yoga through Kalavathi's teacher training, and the teachings of Swami Gitananda changed that. I began to think a lot more about spirituality, both in a general sense and in terms of my own spiritual growth. I started to feel comfortable with words like 'God', 'Divine' and 'spirituality' in ways I hadn't before. My concept of 'God' is not the one I grew up with, it is not the Christian God I am still furious at; it is something far more personal and accessible to me, closer to what I experienced on that seashore during my pregnancy than anything I ever felt in church. I find God in nature, in the sunrise, in the night sky, in the buds on the trees, in the waves that lap on the shore, on the top of a mountain, the laughter of my children, and in the stillness I find on my Yoga mat.

Spirituality is a big factor in successful recovery from addiction. Alcoholics Anonymous talk about the Higher Power, which doesn't have to be 'God' in the Christian sense, but is something you can put your strength in and turn to for comfort (that isn't a bottle of something of course). This might be music, art, physical exercise, writing or any activity that allows a person to turn to it at times when they feel the urge to drink. These outlets give them a connection to their spiritual self.

For me of course, this was Yoga. While I struggled to keep the diary I was supposed to, I found the writing that my Yoga studies required me to do particularly enriching, so much so that I still do on it a regular basis. It is ironic that if I had the understanding of God and spirituality that I have now when I first sought help, I might have been able to cope with the idea of going to AA. Like many people, I imagined it to be all about God in the Christian sense and I didn't feel that was a place for me. Instead Yoga gave me all the spiritual connection I had ever needed and so much more besides. My spiritual development and connection through Yoga came naturally out of what I was learning rather than being told to believe.

I now understand that the lack of spiritual connection to anything other than my vices was a part of why I became addicted. While religious faith doesn't render people immune to addiction, faith does help people to 'weather the storms' that life throws them into. They may find their faith tested and struggle to retain it, but if they do hold tight, it gives them strength to get through terrible adversity. Faith, in its many forms, is the cornerstone of resilience which is something I, and most addicts, are lacking.

Gabor Mate, who works with chronic addicts and has many years of experience of addiction, could be writing for a Yoga text book when he says:

*"Addiction floods in where self-knowledge, and therefore Divine knowledge, are missing. To fil the unendurable void, we become attached to things that cannot possibly compensate us for the loss of who we are."*

An entire chapter of Dr Mate's "In the Realm of Hungry Ghosts" is devoted to the spiritual dimension of addiction and recovery. I have littered it with notes and reference to Yoga philosophy; reading alongside Dr Ananda Balayogi Bhavanani's 'Understanding the Yoga Darshan' is a remarkable juxtaposition of ideas that marry together so well. Both are talking about the effects of lack of spirituality and self-connection and the extremes we go to in order to fill the gap left. I feel that given a lot more time to research, and a greater understanding of scientific research papers, I could write a book on spirituality, and its connection to addiction, recovery and Yoga. Maybe I won't, but I hope someone will. There is a lot that could be written on the subject and I think it would be a very useful book for many people.

If addiction 'floods in where *self-knowledge, and therefore Divine knowledge, are missing,"* then this certainly explains why my year of Yoga training was so effective at helping me into recovery. Yoga is, first and foremost, about connecting us with our spiritual Self, about helping us to see our true identity. This does not happen quickly, but the process of moving towards this knowledge brings many insights, and clear connections to the deeper aspects of us and our connection to the divine. Yoga helps us to look closely without judgement but with compassion at ourselves, to look with love at how we have come to be the person we are today and how we can move forward to be the person we can be tomorrow. Yoga teaches us that we are NOT our body, not our thoughts, not our interactions with the material world. We learn that these are important but they do not define us. Our true identity is not this current incarnation, but the soul that resides in the body. The Yogic belief is that this soul is eternal, has lived in many life forms, and will probably live through many more before we achieve the ultimate goal of Yoga, Enlightenment or liberation. Once we achieve this exalted state we are free from the Karmic cycle of death and rebirth. Of course, one does not have to accept this view if it clashes with religious beliefs, but the importance of the soul is known in all faiths.

Through Yoga we learn to study and get to know ourselves as we are in this current life, while we are much more than the being we are manifested in right now, it is important that we get to know who we are at our core. Yoga and Hinduism teach us that we come into the life form we are in to learn lessons needed to 'burn up' the Karma created in previous lives, and to evolve our soul a little further. This understanding has helped me process all the 'problems' I have experienced in my life so far, as I now see that I needed to experience them to get the lessons I needed. I went through 20 years of addiction so that I would learn what I needed to learn, and boy was there a lot! I can now use this to help others.

This, I believe, is my 'Dharma', my life's purpose. Yoga teaches us that we need to find and live our Dharma in order to evolve our spiritual growth. My experience of addiction and misery makes sense to me if

I can see it as preparation for being able to teach others, and share the path to resilience I have found. It has given me the knowledge and tools to write this book and help people who need help to develop resilience for themselves. Along the journey through my life, I could have taken many different paths, many of which would have made my life easier. Instead though I took the path I did and learned the lessons I learned. I strongly believe that it is my duty, my Dharma, to take those lessons and share them with the wider world in the hope that I am able to help others.

# Stress and addiction

Stress and addiction are close partners in crime. Of course, it is possible to experience high stress without developing any addiction, and addiction doesn't always come directly from stressful experiences, but there are very close links between the two.

Stress can lead us into behaviours that we can become addicted to. Once we are in addiction, the search for the source of the addiction can cause stress, as can the withdrawal symptoms. The two states feed each other continuously, a truly destructive symbiotic relationship that goes on within our mind, but that we feel utterly powerless to control.

Stress is an incredibly powerful force within us which exercises tremendous control over our physical and emotional state. It is an evolutionary necessity, a vital function of the nervous system designed to help us deal with life or death situations, such as a threat to our life. When we encounter, or think we have encountered, a threat that affects our safety, our sympathetic nervous system (fight or flight) is activated.

The brain sends signals to the nervous system that there is a threat and various hormones are produced these include adrenaline, cortisol, glucagon, aldosterone and noradrenaline. Combined they create the stressed state in the body and mind.

They give us a quick burst of energy so that we can flee to escape.

They lower our pain threshold so we can fight or run even if injured.

They increase the blood flow and heart rate so that the blood is circulating around the muscles faster, enabling them to function better.

They widen air the passages in the lungs which allows us to take in more oxygen with each breath.

They widen the pupils to allow greater sensory perception.

They raise the blood pressure and glucose level in the blood stream.

These responses are designed to meet the needs of the individual to deal with a clear and present threat. Swami Gitananda uses the example of a sabre toothed tiger. An ancient man encountering a sabre toothed tiger would have had a very real threat posed to him. His stress response would have caused him to flee, freeze, or fight; he would have either killed the tiger, fled from the tiger, or the tiger would have killed him. One way or another, the stress response would have only been needed for a short space of time. Provided he survived the encounter, he would return to a calm state of mind and body. The parasympathetic nervous system (rest and digest mode) would return, maintaining the balance of his body.

Unfortunately for modern man, the stress response happens whether the threat is real or imagined. Our brain responds to a perceived threat as though it is real. In our western culture we no longer have to worry about sabre toothed tigers attacking us or any other daily peril. The brain and nervous system do not know this though. Our perception shapes our reality, not the other way around.

Our minds are bombarded with information from our senses all the time. We cannot possibly process all this information but our subconscious mind does. It takes nano seconds for the mind to work out whether we need to deal with a situation immediately or if it can be left in the subconscious.

We experience stressful experiences in everyday life and our body and mind reacts accordingly. For example, we are all familiar with the feeling of fear that we get when walking through a dark lane. This is a helpful time to be aware, there might actually be danger lurking in the shadows. Most of the time though it is simply our fear that something might be there that creates the stress response.

Road rage has become a modern day phenomenon but it is another example of these innate survival instincts. Take the following common situation; a driver gets cut up, the incident could have resulted in an accident, but it didn't. The driver perceives the threat and his body reacts. His heart rate escalates and his blood pressure rises. The accident didn't happen though and all this pent up energy has nowhere to go. The driver is filled with fury instead and becomes engaged (hence the term road-rage).

The consequences for anyone living life at this level of stress are very damaging. A body and mind cannot be healthy and well when under massive pressure. In Yoga there is a concept known as Adhi-Vyadhi that tells us that there is a very deep connection that exists between the mind and the body. If we do not deal with problems in the mind they will manifest in the body. We can all recognise that when we feel stressed it affects our ability to eat, to sleep and to relax but the effects are even deeper. Our sensitivity to pain and other sense information are impacted as our endocrine system keeps us permanently in 'flight or fight' mode, it affects the heart rate, the respiratory system and our blood pressure. The medical profession recognize that stress is a major contributing factor in conditions such as asthma, IBS, heart disease, stroke to name but a few.

In the workplace, stress is the 3rd highest cause of absence. I would suggest that the true figure of this is actually far higher, as stress is likely to be a factor in a large proportion of musculoskeletal, minor, back pain and drink or drug related issues, as well as the 'non genuine' absences. There is a stigma associated with stress, particularly in the workplace – fear of losing one's job might mean that 'stress' is not actually admitted to as reasons for absence. I know in my own case, I rarely admitted I wasn't in work due to stress, I invented reasons for my absence but wouldn't admit that I was struggling to cope.

Some types of stress are beneficial if controlled appropriately. If we have an impending deadline, we have to be stressed enough to focus on the task, but if the stress levels get too high it actually impedes concentration because we become consumed with what might go wrong if we don't meet the deadline. In this situation our attention is drawn to the negative and any problems we perceive get bigger and bigger.

Stress, and our ability to deal with it, is a major factor in the development of addiction. The sheer scale of the addiction problem in Western society and the range of addictions demonstrate the result of people's unprecedented and unmanaged stress levels. There is an increasing body of addiction research that are looking at the effects of addiction on the mind, the factors that make addiction more likely, and the factors that influence and promote recovery.

*At this point, I would like to reiterate the point I made in the introduction of this book. I am not a scientist. I have not been trained to read, evaluate and understand scientific papers, and while I have managed to make some connections in my understanding of the science behind addiction, I am not confident in my ability to explain it well. There is as much skill involved in communicating scientific ideas as there is in understanding them. I would dearly love to be able to research the links between stress, addiction and Yoga, to look at the science at work; it is my hope that one day I will be able to do this*

# Desperately seeking something

Throughout my life, I have developed a wide range of addictions to various substances, people and behaviours. Obsessions with certain bands, unrequited 'love', a dysfunctional attitude towards sex, eating disorders, digital technology and my much written about addiction to alcohol, cigarettes and marijuana. Many people can enjoy these things without developing addictive behaviours – so why did I develop addictions?

Some would say that my addictions suggest a weakness in my personality or that I am a bad, immoral and flawed person. Neuroscience tells me I have an illness that can never be cured. It is true that while I have been able to combat my addiction to cigarettes and alcohol, I do still display addictive tendencies, such as sugar cravings, occasional coffee binges and that most modern of addictions, internet addiction.

Alcohol was initially my way of shielding myself from the world and how I saw myself. It became a tool I used to self-medicate for a mental illness I had never tried to get professional help with. Whether alcohol caused the mental illness, or was caused by it, I do not know, it is a classic 'chicken and egg' situation. I never made it to the diagnosis stage of my journey with mental health services. I started the process of referral a short while before I started Yoga teacher training. But I didn't pursue this medical route as by the time my referral came through I had begun to find salvation through Yoga, but I often wonder if I should have continued my referral anyway. I don't recommend anyone cuts out the medical professionals from their recovery. It worked for me but it was a very risky decision to make. Had I continued with the process, I am sure I would have been diagnosed with something. I have seen myself described in the symptoms of number of conditions, all of which are known to increase propensity to addiction and dependence.

Addiction needs to be looked at in terms of what is happening in the brain of the addict at all stages of the addiction process. I will use alcohol and my own experience as an example to illustrate the science as I understand it. Although difference substances and activities trigger different responses in some parts of the brain, the process towards addiction is the same.

When I had that first drink of alcohol at 16 and enjoyed that feeling of increased relaxation, confidence, and self-esteem that was the Dopamine Reward Pathway in action. The information that booze helped me to feel good was filed away and stored for future use. Dopamine is a neurotransmitter that tells us when something is good for us and we should do it again. It is vital for survival of the individual and the species; it is why sex feels good, after all we need to do it a lot to increase the likelihood of procreation. We enjoy food for the same reason. Dopamine is involved in the production of breast milk to keep mothers feeding their babies (and why I still miss being able to feed my kids that way). Substances such as alcohol, cocaine and other drugs, as well as activities we get pleasure from also trigger the production of dopamine, or mimic its effects, meaning that these activities make us feel good, feel connected to others and allow us the escape we are seeking. Therefore, when we feel the need to feel good, our brain reminds us that that substance or behaviour made us feel good and we seek it out again.

As I grew up, I found myself becoming more and more depressed. I was consumed with a sense of shame at things I had done in my life, and thought myself to be a terrible person. This overwhelming feeling of shame meant I wanted to feel better about myself and to find a way to escape from the inner torture. My brain knew the answer of course.

Have a drink; that will make you feel good!

Have a cigarette; that will make you feel good!

Drugs will make you feel good!

Go and find someone to sleep with that will make you feel loved and loveable!

Loud music will make you feel good! Don't worry that you have neighbours, they can't hear it!

Chocolate will make you feel good!

Every time I indulged in any of these substances or behaviours, the dopamine flooded into my brain, and I did feel good, for a while. However, it didn't last long and I soon felt bad again, worse than I had done before. I had been delaying dealing with the negative feelings properly, instead I now had to deal with the post dopamine comedown as well. Of course now I felt bad and wanted to feel good so cravings would begin in earnest.

The dopamine reward pathway, when artificially stimulated, reminds me of Audrey from the Little Shop of Horrors, a comparison also made by Dr Mate in 'In the Realm of Hungry Ghosts'.

In that film, Audrey II, the carnivorous plant, appears to be dying until Seymour accidentally feeds it a drop of his blood and realises that Audrey thrives on blood. As she gets stronger, her need for blood increases and she makes more and more demands on Seymour, promising him the world if he helps her. Feeding Audrey II takes Seymour down increasingly dark paths as he is manipulated into acts that he knows are morally and legally wrong, but he is powerless in the face of Audrey II's hold over him. Eventually, that powerlessness costs him his life and the life of the woman he loves.

As Dr Mate tells us, 'addiction consumes, first the self, then the others within its orbit'.

Such is how addiction develops. As the artificially increased dopamine leads us to feel happier, and more pleasure, it also creates more stress, and leaves the individual increasingly sensitive to stress and with a reduced ability to experience 'normal' routes to enjoyment. The stress caused by the cycle of craving, acquisition, withdrawal takes the addicted person to more and more extreme levels of behaviour as they are forced to do anything necessary to feed the addiction.

I can see that as my addiction developed, this was manifesting itself in me. If at a social occasion where I couldn't drink, I wouldn't really be able to relax and enjoy it. I would invariably have to know that there was alcohol at home waiting for me, or that I would be able to buy some on the way home regardless of what time I would be arriving home.

Addiction is a slow process that you don't really notice until you try to gain any sort of control. The shock of realising you are addicted can be hard to accept, I remember being adamant for years that I wasn't addicted to nicotine, thinking I couldn't be because I didn't experience cravings for cigarettes when I was with my parents (when I couldn't, or didn't think I could, smoke), so I couldn't possibly be addicted. The first time I tried to quit was a complete revelation for me, I got completely freaked out and drained by how hard it was and gave up trying. On another occasion I had managed to go about a week without smoking ahead of national 'No Smoking Day'. This was the latest in a long line of attempts to give up, prompted as usual by the knowledge that as an asthmatic, smoking was the most absurd and life threatening thing for me to do. I had managed this week just fine, but was starting to wane in my ability to resist the cravings. When I came across an information stand at college about No Smoking Day, my resolve collapsed beneath me as I contemplated leaflets saying 'quit for good' or words to that effect, and the thought of never being able to smoke again became too much for me. I burst into tears, left the college reception area and went straight to the shop for a pack of 10!

This is Selye's General Adaptation Syndrome in effect. The **alarm** I felt at the harm I was causing to myself made me really want to quit, but the effort involved was too hard, **resistance** kicked in leading to **exhaustion** and the inevitable relapse.

In order to break free of my addictions, I needed to do more than simply stop drinking or stop smoking. I had emotional attachments to the sources of my addictions that became stronger whenever I tried to just stop. When I tried to tell myself that I wasn't going to drink I could guarantee that something would happen that day that would make drinking 'essential'. I needed find a way to deal with the emotional and mental attachments I had to alcohol. I needed to develop resilience to be able to deal with everyday problems without alcohol.

Relapse is a very real threat to recovering addicts. Alcoholics Anonymous tells its members that they will remain alcoholics for their whole lives and must be ever vigilant against the possibility of relapse. While I don't accept the notion that I will always be an alcoholic, I understand the thinking behind this.

Recovery is dependent on many factors, many of which are internal to the recovering alcoholic. Recovery capital is the term used to describe these factors. They include social, personal, physical and cultural factors, factors such as employment, housing, support, community, coping strategies and personal resilience.

Addicts need to be helped to develop recovery capital. Resilience is something that develops through our experience of life, but we can learn tools that can help us to develop better resilience and coping strategies. I shall look into some of these later in this book.

When I was deep into my addiction, I had very little personal resilience, no inner resources to deal with life beyond 'I'm stressed/uneasy/insecure, therefore I must drink'. Reacting to life with anger and frustration, turning to alcohol, drugs or cigarettes to deal with it was my default. Until I was able to develop this resilience, I was never going to be able to simply stop drinking, getting through life without my 'coping strategies' was unthinkable.

The Welsh Government's Recovery Framework defines recovery thus:

*'Recovery from problematic drug or alcohol use is defined as a process in which the difficulties associated with substance misuse are eliminated or significantly reduced, and the resulting personal improvement becomes sustainable.'*

The process described in this definition includes the need for very practical support including secure housing and such like but it places a lot of emphasis on the development of personal strengths and inner resources. This is where Yoga can be incredibly valuable.

# Yoga for Recovery Capital

Through Yoga it is possible to learn to control the stress response that makes recovery from addiction so hard. Yoga offers us tools to help us control reactions to stressful situations and to choose the better response. It can help with the difficulties recovering addicts have with sleep. It can help people to accept who they are and to come to terms with, or change, the aspects of themselves that they find unbearable. It can create resilience that might not otherwise exist.

Yoga has been proven to impact positively on the mood, stress levels, relaxation, the ability to sleep, and the ability to stay sober following a recovery programme[1].

Streeter et al (2007) found that Yoga sessions can increase GABA levels in the brain by up to 27%[2]. GABA is a neurotransmitter, which reduces energy levels and has a calming effect on the mind. It is an ingredient in sedatives such as Xanax and Valium. Low GABA rates have been linked to anxiety and mood disorders. Increasing this substance naturally in the brain through Yoga can improve participants' state of mind considerably.

Yoga is able to target stress related cognition, emotions and the cravings that cause so many in recovery to relapse. The skills, insights and self-awareness gained through Yoga and its associated 'mindfulness' practices can target multiple psychological, neural,

---

[1] http://www.ncbi.nlm.nih.gov/pubmed/23642957
[2] http://www.ncbi.nlm.nih.gov/pubmed/17532734

physiological and behavioural processes implicated in recovery and relapse.

Addiction often stems from, and causes, very negative self-image. This can create a spiral of negative emotions that fuels the addiction. Yoga teaches people to view themselves and the world with compassion and not judgement. This shift in perception can be hugely transformative to the addict in recovery.

Yoga also promotes gratitude and encourages people to be grateful for and to look for the positives in life as oppose to focusing on the negatives. This is a very powerful new world view and one that can very quickly lead to a more positive outlook.

Research carried out by the American National Institute on Drug Abuse (NIDA) found that people use drugs (and other substances or behaviours) for 4 main reasons – to feel good, to feel better, to do better, and because others are doing it. It is ironic that these eventually become the exact same reasons that people want to quit and break free of their addictions. Ultimately, the promises these substances and behaviours offer us turn out to be hollow and they deliver the exact opposite – they promise self-esteem but they destroy what little we have. They promise confidence but they leave us paranoid and fearful. They promise creativity and leave our brains unable to function. They promise oblivion but the internal voices of dissent and loathing just grow louder.

Addiction begins long before we take that first drink, that first smoke, that first line, that first comforting bar of chocolate, or the first time we remove our clothes for a stranger just to feel the comforting touch of another human. Addiction is the manifestation of brain development and patterns of behaviour that usually starts in childhood. I am choosing not to go deeply into this subject for this book. I am mindful that many people have experienced far deeper pain than I can ever imagine and I don't think I am knowledgeable or experienced enough in this to offer anything other than a clumsy regurgitation of other people's ideas. I would urge anyone who has any interest in this area, in particular those who work with addicts in any capacity, to read the work of experts such as Dr Gabor Mate. When we approach addiction as a survival mechanism that develops to enable people to survive in the face of emotional turmoil, we can see people with addictions in a far more sympathetic light than stereotypical media portrayal and political rhetoric invites.

Addiction is a massive public health crisis on a global scale and as long as decisions and policies are made that treat addicts as the problem, rather than helping them to resolve their problems it will only get worse.

# Why the pain?

Addiction is a symptom of underlying pain and suffering. Gabor Mate encourages us to ask not 'Why is there addiction?' when we look at trying to understand addiction, but 'Why the pain?'. You only need to read a few chapters of 'In the Realm of Hungry Ghosts', or of Johann Hari's 'Chasing the Scream', or talk to anyone who has had experience of addiction to know that addiction IS suffering. It is born out of suffering, it creates suffering, and the only way to tackle it is by confronting the source of suffering head on.

Addiction develops when a person needs to find a way to escape from emotional pain. A huge proportion of substance addicts experienced severe trauma during childhood. This is a useful insight to remember when we look at the plight of abused children. If those children don't receive the support and care they need during childhood, there is a really good chance they will turn to harmful substances and behaviour to block out their pain when they are older.

Through the process of writing this book, I have come to realise that there are many similarities between the road to recovery from addiction, and the path of spiritual growth. Both are very difficult paths for anyone to take. Both are aimed at achieving freedom. Yoga as a spiritual path aims for freedom of the soul, through recovery we aim to free ourselves from the grip of an all-consuming, life threatening addiction.

Along the path to spiritual growth and addiction recovery there are many obstacles that can trip a person up. These obstacles come not from external influences, but from the mind. Georg Feuerstein, in his audio lessons 'The Lost Secrets of Yoga' tells us 'we cannot become happy, we can only be happy'. Happiness is entirely within our control. That is not to say we can control all aspects of our life but we can choose how to respond to them.

Viktor Frankl knew a thing or two about suffering intolerable injustice and cruelty. He was imprisoned for 3 years in a Nazi concentration camp and saw friends and family suffer and die at the hands of their captors. He could have been forgiven for falling into a pit of despair. However, he recognised that while the Nazis could take his possessions, his physical freedom, his food and those he loved from him, they could not take the freedom of his mind. His widely respected 'Man's Search for Meaning', while being a very traumatic and difficult read is an incredible account of what the human race is capable of, both its cruelty and its strength. Not only can we endure pain but we can survive mentally as well as physically.

*"Everything can be taken from a man but one thing: the last of the human freedoms—to choose one's attitude in any given set of circumstances, to choose one's own way."*

This Frankl quote speaks volumes about the man but also gives us a great lesson in the power of our thoughts.

One of the great lessons yoga teaches us is how to not let our thoughts control our actions. This is something that I used to struggle with a lot. Living in a constant state of stress and anxiety, I would focus intensely on the source of stress, and allow that stress to build up in my mind until I could think of nothing else. Inevitably, this would lead to me being in such an agitated state that the only hope I had of getting out of it was to buy wine, cigarettes and often marijuana. These would 'help' to relive the stress, but would, of course, inevitably lead to more stress and anxiety.

Since I no longer drink or smoke I don't struggle with so much stress and anxiety. This is the ultimate chicken and egg situation; I have never quite worked out if my reduced stress resulted in my ability to give up my addictions or if giving up my addictions released me from the stress. I suspect it is a circular cause and effect pattern, the two factors work together inclusively. As I developed resilience through the practices I was engaging with, and the new way I was living, I was living in a calmer state of mind in general, and I also had a range of tools to turn to when stress did occur.

I realised with a pleasant shock recently, after one of the most stressful days I have had in a long time that I hadn't even thought for one second about reaching for booze or fags. If there was ever a day I was going to find my sobriety tested it was that day. "Old" Esther would have felt utterly justified in buying wine and cigarettes, even though doing so would make a difficult situation worse. "New" Esther didn't think about it. I was in bed that night and it suddenly dawned on me, and the thought didn't make me want to indulge, as it might have done before, it made me even happier with sobriety.

**I think, therefore that is how it is.**

The thoughts we allow ourselves to dwell on are so crucial to our wellbeing, or lack of it. Our reality is entirely shaped by our perceptions of the world. If I think I am having a bad day, I probably am. If I think I am having a good day, the same is true. We must remember too that our perceptions are _entirely unique_ to us. What is true for me is not necessarily true for you. I might find a situation intolerable that another person might take happily in their stride. Yoga recognises our uniqueness, and teaches us to see past this. Through practices such as Pratipaksha Bhavanam, which I will explain later, we learn that we can actually control the thoughts in our mind, or at least, we can choose what thoughts we focus on.

A few years ago, I gave up smoking for six months. I had used 'magic giving up smoking pills', as I called them, and had found the process so easy that colleagues in the job I started the day I gave up didn't even know I was an ex-smoker until about 4 months in to the role. When the organisation started going through some big problems, I stayed off the cigarettes until one day when it all got too much for me. I was driving home and got caught in lots of traffic.

'I am so glad' I thought to myself, 'that I don't smoke any more. If I did, I would have probably had 2 by now!'

Fatal thought.

Within 5 minutes, smoking cigarettes was all I could think about. I could taste, smell, feel, even see that cigarette in my mouth and hand. I had to have one. I got myself so upset and strung out that I was picturing driving straight into the vehicle in front of me. I realised what was happening, and acknowledged that I had to allow myself to decide to buy cigarettes to avoid creating a rush hour pile up! As soon as I made that decision, I calmed down. That first cigarette tasted so good, but I had tears of shame and frustration rolling down my face as I smoked it.

The desire for that cigarette was a very powerful thought that created a scary reality for me. I was in a state of great distress at the time it was the same year as my break~~down~~through. I was very fragile mentally and emotionally at this time and it scares me to think of the power of a momentary suicidal thought.

## Pratipaksha Bhavanam

As we can see, when we focus on a thought, it becomes very real to us. It can affect our moods, our emotions, our actions, our mental well-being and even our physical health and safety! Yoga has known for a very long time of the strong connection between the mind and the body, or Adhi Vyadhi, and modern science is now coming to see that too.

If we focus on a negative thought, that negativity becomes the lens through which we view the world.

Pratipaksha Bhavanam is the act of replacing the negative with the positive. The more we develop awareness of our thoughts, the more we can change them and stop them from dictating how we live our life. Had I known about this when I was in that traffic jam, I might not have been so beaten by my need for a cigarette!

This is something that has been hugely beneficial in helping me to completely change my life. I never thought it would be possible to get through life's stresses without turning to alcohol to deal with it. Now sobriety is completely normal and I can't imagine doing anything else.

Pratipaksha Bhavanam is about replacing negative thoughts with positive ones. So instead of thinking 'I'm such a f***ing idiot' (one of my former 'favourites') I catch myself and turn that thought around - so my thoughts get replaced with 'I'm not an idiot, I sometimes make mistakes but learn from them, I'm trying my best and I'm a good person'. If you can't quite manage that, a shake of the head and a stern 'STOP IT!' to yourself can be effective. Stop the thought and find something else to focus on.

Try to really notice when you have negative thoughts in your head, and whenever you spot them, turn them into something positive. This can be related to negativity about yourself, other people, situations and such like. I used this to help me make better choices, so at the start of my sober journey, I occasionally might think I wanted a cigarette or a drink, but I would turn that around and remind myself how much I enjoy not drinking and smoking, how much nicer it is to wake up in the morning with a clear head, a full memory, and a mouth that doesn't taste like the carpet in a pub!

This practice can be used to change any habit or behaviour, but it must become a habit in itself. You must develop an awareness of your thoughts, and learn to recognise the negative self-talk when you do it. The best way to do this is through the breath. I will discuss both awareness and the breath in more detail in later chapters.

## The Yogic view of suffering

While many of the obstacles that cause relapse in addiction recovery seem to come from other places, at their core, they are all connected to the 5 obstacles that Patanjali highlighted for us. Patanjali called these Pancha Kleshas. A study of the Kleshas can shed some light on the problems faced in addiction as surely as they help us light the path to spiritual growth.

These Kleshas are:

*Avidya* – ignorance of the True Self, the Divine, which leads to...

*Asmita* – egoism, identification only with the physical existence, with the labels we give ourselves and that others give us. The ego becomes caught up in...

*Raga* – attraction, desires for external objects, happiness in things, experiences and other people and...

*Dwesha* – repulsion to external objects, fear.

The other 4 Kleshas all contribute to *Abinivesha*, the urge to survive, to preserve the physical body at all costs.

## Avidya

What we experience as happiness in fleeting moments in our daily lives can actually lead to more suffering because we want the happy feeling to last and it simply can't. Patanjali believed that the origin of unhappiness was ignorance or Avidya, that we cannot be truly happy until we connect with our eternal Self. This forms a stark contrast to the Western saying 'Ignorance is Bliss'. I find this a fascinating contradiction. It is particularly interesting as the word 'Bliss' is often used in Yoga to refer to the state of enlightenment.

The life of the addict is a perfect example of this. Stuck on a wheel of suffering, the source of the addiction offers brief respite. That is, until the craving and need for that source returns, along with the negative emotions that we think the addiction is protecting us from. We think that we are escaping from our problems or finding brief happiness in oblivion but the unhappiness is always there and returns stronger and louder.

In a later chapter on the Niyamas, I will be exploring the benefits of Swadhyaya, or self-study. It is through this that we gain the self-knowledge that allows us to eradicate Avidya from our lives. Patanjali teaches us that Avidya, as the root of the other Kleshas, is also the key to their destruction. If we free ourselves of the ignorance of Avidya, truly embrace the knowledge of the Divine Self and live accordingly, then the other Kleshas will just fall away and we will reach the state of Moksha, or freedom.

Patanjali's clear message is that if we live in ignorance, we will never reach the higher states of being that is the aim of conscious evolution, and we will never achieve true happiness. By removing our ignorance of the Self, and connecting with who we really are, our True, Divine self, we can achieve this state of true happiness.

## Asmita

Because we don't know our true Self, we identify with the 'I' we have created for ourselves. This is a reflection of how we perceive the world and our place in it based on our interpretations of the information our senses pick up. We become attached to this identity and this false sense of who we are. We become fearful of anything that challenges this. What we fear, we fight, so we will resist any indication that we need to change.

This makes change challenging for everyone, but for the addict, who has carefully constructed an identity in which he is shielded from pain by the addiction, it can be especially hard. Even when we want to see past this identity, the pathways in the brain have been well established and breaking them is difficult. The addict will ask themselves, 'Who am I if I am not drunk, how do I interact with the world without my shield to protect me?'

## Raga

Raga is seeking out objects of desire; the seeking of short term pleasure over what is good for us. This is the klesha of the dopamine reward pathway, of craving, of that desire so strong we will do anything to appease it. We learn that something feels good so we want more of it. The problem with Raga is that the desire for the pleasurable means that we don't usually stop at the one pleasurable thing, when we like something, we want it again. So, using alcohol as an example, one drink turns into a night of heavy drinking, and can, in the 'right' circumstances, develop into alcoholism.

It is very easy to see how Raga arises out of an ego built on ignorance. "I want it, I like it, I deserve it, so I will have it". With a greater understanding of the Divine Self and a reduced ego, we can see past our desires, and seek only that which is good for us.

## Dwesha

Dwesha is an instinctive repulsion from something that causes us pain. It is the opposite of Raga, but they are opposite like two sides of the same coin, the same but different. Dwesha comes from our animal instincts; it is very closely linked to our survival instincts. Survival instincts are vital in the animal and young child, if we wish to evolve we must learn to rise above them and not react with fear or repulsion to something that might cause pain or discomfort. I, like many others, turned to alcohol because normal reality was at times unbearable and I felt far more comfortable escaping. This escape gave me momentary release from the emotional pain I felt it only caused greater suffering in the long term.

If we are trying to grow, either to escape an addiction, or to progress spiritually, we must move beyond this desire to escape. We cannot always avoid the things that we don't like, any more than we can fill our lives with nothing but the things that bring us pleasure. We have to experience the 'bad' and 'good' in life in order to learn, and to fully experience life.

## Abhinivesha

Abhinivesha is 'fear of death'. It is the hardest Klesha to break free from because it is a deep rooted instinctual response shared by all living creatures, it forms the basis of our survival instincts. As has already been mentioned, a strong survival instinct is vital in animals and in new born babies, but in evolved into humans it is a real obstacle to enlightenment.

In my contemplation of the Kleshas and reading into the nature of addiction, I was struck that our addictions develop their own Abhinivesha. Like Audrey II in The Little Shop of Horrors, our addictions will do anything to survive and will take us down with them. They lead us to behaviours we know are harming us on every level, harming those we love and our wider community. In the face of the determined efforts of the addiction to survive, it takes a massive amount of work for us to rise about them. It takes work, but it is not impossible.

## Destroying the Kleshas, achieving freedom, through Yoga

Patanjali tells us how we can destroy the Kleshas and reach the enlightenment that is our goal. It is not an easy task, and may take more than one lifetime to achieve, but it is possible through following the steps laid out in the 8 Limbs of Yoga. We can use the same tools to rise above the addiction that blights us. The good news is this can be achieved in one lifetime!

In order to achieve full, sustainable recovery and control of our animal instincts we must refine the higher human practices through adherence to the Yamas and Niyamas. All the Yamas and Niyamas are important to practice if we are to attain full recovery. We must stop harming ourselves and others, we must learn to be truthful, we must learn to think about the purity of what we put into our bodies.

Patanjali tells us that the main key stone to destruction of the Kleshas is through Kriya Yoga. This is the dedicated practice of the final three Niyamas of Yoga, Tapas, Swadhyaya and Ishwara Pranidhana; discipline and concentration, deep self-study, and surrender to the Divine. Through this commitment to Kriya Yoga, and only through this, can we truly destroy the Kleshas and find true enlightenment.

It is easy to see how this can be applied to recovery from addiction, and how Kriya Yoga as a way of life can help us to free ourselves from addiction and retain that freedom. If we apply ourselves with discipline, look into ourselves with compassion, care for our bodies and surrender our actions to a higher power (whatever that means to us), we can free ourselves from addiction. There are massive similarities here between Kriya Yoga and several steps of the 12 Step Recovery model. The Yamas and Niyamas are Yoga's 'steps' they were my steps to my own recovery, and they could be yours as well!

# Awareness and Judgement

If Yoga is a way of integrating all aspects of our life together, then we need to start by developing awareness. We cannot begin to improve or change anything unless we know where we are. Yoga helps us to gently take ourselves apart and put ourselves back together again, leaving out the bits that don't work. This is certainly what I did and the first step was to look closely at who I was, something I had avoided for years by hiding behind alcohol.

The Yoga path is not an easy one to tread; there may be a lot of pain along the way as we begin to discover long hidden truths about ourselves. It is important that we do this inquiry into ourselves with compassion and kindness for ourselves, and the ability to reach out for support when our discoveries become so painful that we can't move forward. I had several moments through my searching when I didn't feel that I wanted to carry on with it as the revelations were difficult to bear. Ultimately though, pursuit of the discoveries eventually led me to release and healing, but I did need friends, family and my new Yoga family to lean on.

Yoga teaches us that we are one with the rest of the creation. Through living a yogic life, we can develop clear awareness of this one-ness, instead of feeling that we are separate from everything else. This feeling of separation is what drives much of our unhappiness; our disconnection from nature and each other is the root cause of the biggest evils in the world.

Yoga has been described as 'Conscious Evolution'. In order to live a yogic life, you have to embark on a voyage of personal evolution with consciousness. You have to be actively aware of where you have started from, what you hope to achieve, and each new, often very subtle, development on the journey.

This requires awareness and it is known as the 'Four Fold Awareness'.

The first stage of this awareness is consciousness of the body; of what the body needs and what it is doing. This is where we begin to notice our unconscious habits. It means noticing the breath, noticing movement, being aware of speech and all the body's natural activities. It means taking care of our physical selves and ensuring that good nutrition and hydration is provided. We need to keep our bodies well rested and exercised so that sufficient oxygen is allowed to enter the system and that waste products can be efficiently removed. It also means not inflicting harmful substances or practices to damage the body, so alcohol, caffeine, processed food and sugars, polluted air, water and food should be avoided or minimised.

The more we pay attention to the body, the more we become attuned to its needs. I believe that this is part of what happened with me; before I stopped drinking I was taking greater care of my body, and paying more attention to it. This meant I became increasingly aware of the negative impact drinking was having on me compared to the way my body and mind felt when I didn't drink. This comparison was a very big influence – why would I choose to do something that made me feel so awful, when I had other tools at my disposal to deal with my emotions, and could experience my mind and body feeling so much healthier.

It is very important that we develop this awareness objectively, and that we do not judge ourselves as we notice things. The same is true for our judgement of others; Yoga and happiness are 'judgement free zones'.

The second stage of the Four Fold Awareness is an awareness of the tremendous power the emotions hold over the physical wellbeing of the body. When we know the extent to which negative emotions have a harmful effect on the body, and vice versa, then we can take action to limit the negative and embrace, encourage and enhance the positive.

Negative emotions vary in the intensity of the harmful effects on the body. Envy, jealousy, hate, greed, malice and possessiveness are the most damaging emotions, while embarrassment, aversion, fear and escapism are secondary. With practice, you can develop sufficient awareness to notice when these emotions start to rise and control them. Without this awareness most people are controlled by them. The old adage of 'take a deep breath and count to ten' can sometimes be all that is needed, sometimes maybe a longer count is called for.

From my own personal experience, it also helps greatly to realise that one cannot control everyone, or every situation one finds oneself in. Sometimes you just have to let things be as they are, pick your battles wisely and not take things too personally.

The third stage of the Four Fold Awareness is an awareness of the mind. In particular the effects that the mind has on emotions and in turn the body. If the mind is allowed to dwell on a negative thought this will turn into a negative emotion. Through regular yoga practices, including asanas, pranayama, and awareness, we can gain a new attentive perspective of the mind, which can lead to a higher connection.

The fourth stage of the Four Fold Awareness is Samadhi, or Enlightenment. This is 'awareness of awareness', and is the ultimate aim of Yoga, true connection with the Divine, although we may still be many lifetimes from achieving this.

**Developing this awareness is a deep practice in itself, but an incredibly rewarding one.**

**Throughout your day, stop and notice your breath, notice the way your body moves, notice the thoughts that pass through your mind. Really notice it, notice every aspect of the movement, action, thought. When you find an emotion rising up in you, notice it, reflect on it. Do this without judgement, there is no good and bad in awareness, there is only awareness. When you notice an aspect of your behaviour, thoughts, words that you dislike, simply allow the observation to settle, do not 'beat yourself up' about it. I am painfully aware of how much I swear and I don't like it anymore. Years of this unconscious habit is hard to eliminate completely, but with constant awareness, the amount I swear is now much reduced, and continues to reduce further.**

I recommend writing and journaling as a way to record your observations on yourself. At the end of each day, spend some time looking back on your day and reflect on things that happened, not simply listing events that occurred through the day, but thinking about why you acted the way you did, why you said things you said, why you thought the things you did. This is a good practice to develop, and I would recommend you get into the practice of keeping some sort of diary or journal as you progress along your journey through life.

As an initial exercise to help you reflect on where you are at the start of your journey, a good practice is to write an essay or letter to yourself. In the first month's teacher training 'homework' we had to write an essay entitled 'Who am I?' This was a fantastic start to my journey of self-discovery; I had a few revelations about myself during this essay alone.

If you wish to do this, I recommend you sit down with a sheet of paper and a pen, and just write. You could either write an essay with the same title I had, or maybe write a letter of introduction to someone (a pretend someone of course). If someone else was writing a letter of introduction to you, what would they write? These thoughts should always honest and non-judgemental. Bear in mind that if someone was doing this, they would not focus on your faults, but would tell another person about your good qualities as well. If you are going to do this exercise, it is important that you don't only focus on the bits of yourself that you don't like, find the positive and be kind about the 'negative'. If you struggle to find the positive, find someone who you know cares about you and ask them. Sometimes we struggle to see the likeable parts of ourselves so it helps to get someone else's perspective.

Becoming aware of our thoughts, breath, movement, actions and motivations can lead us to identify area that we need or want to change. It is important that you don't judge yourself for these areas. You have been living unconsciously for most of your life, you are at the start of a journey to wake up, forgive yourself for your 'faults', and know that you can improve almost every aspect of yourself with conscious effort.

This is just the first step of the journey. If you were embarking on a mountain hike, you wouldn't berate yourself for not being at the top when you have just left your house would you?

The journey to a Yoga life can be likened to a mountain hike in other ways; it is work, it takes time, requires dedication and deep breaths, it can make you want to turn back and give up, but if you persevere, the views along the way are spectacular and the journey full of joy, wonder and reasons to be happy. We are going to take this journey together and not worry about the destination.

# Yamas and Niyamas

The foundation of Patanjali's Eight Limbs of Yoga are the Yamas and Niyamas. These are often referred to as the moral and ethical restraints. They are the bedrock of a good solid Yoga practice; we cannot really claim to be 'practising Yoga' if we do the physical work, the Asana and the Pranayama, but ignore the Yamas and Niyamas.

Dr Ananda Balayogi Bhavanani, Swami Gitananda's son, says in 'Understanding the Yoga Darshan' that 'the greatest joy and growth comes in the effort'. It is very hard in the modern Western world to attain perfection in these Yamas and Niyamas but it is not impossible, and the lack of perfection doesn't mean that we shouldn't try. We gain lots when we try to live according to the Yamas and Niyamas; every effort towards them brings great rewards.

The Yamas and Niyamas do not exist in isolation; they are very interdependent but they feed each other. For example, at the start of my training, I was a vegetarian, and considered that I was acting in a way that was ethical and humane. I did not believe that animals were suffering so that I could eat the cheese omelettes that I loved so much. Through contemplation of Ahimsa (non-harming), armed with a little *knowledge* about the treatment of animals in the dairy industry, I came to see (through Swadhyaya) that in order to be true to my values (Satya), to ensure I was eating clean food (Saucha), and not causing harm (Ahimsa) or taking what is not mine to take (Asteya), I needed to change to a plant based diet. Sticking to this diet requires control of cravings (Brahmacharya) and discipline (Tapas), but is worth it as I now feel that my diet reflects my values.

This approach can be applied to all aspects of life. Contemplation of the Yamas and Niyamas helps me to be a better mother, a better home maker, a better teacher. They are all about helping us become better on all levels of our being, and if we do nothing but try to live according to these values, we are living Yoga at a very high level indeed.

While the Yamas and Niyamas can influence how we act and think, they also apply to what we allow others to do to us. If, for example, I leave something of value in an unlocked car and it gets stolen, I must take responsibility for this and accept that I allowed this to happen. The Yamas and Niyamas protect us from falling into victim mode and encourage us to remember that we are 100% responsible for our lives.

## Yamas

The Yamas help us to move beyond our base animal nature, help us to function better in society and overcome urges based on our survival instinct. As conscious human beings, we are capable of going further than mere survival. The survival instinct is strong in us all but it does not need to be the force that drives our behaviour

### Ahimsa

Ahimsa means non-violence. This is commonly translated as non-harming. This means that you should endeavour to make sure that your actions, words and thoughts do no harm another. At its most obvious level this means not committing acts of violence on another, and this is why many Yoga practitioners are vegetarian or vegan.

Beyond this, Ahimsa means not hurting another with your words, trying to control your thoughts, not sitting in judgement of others, not spreading hurtful gossip and avoiding harm, for example, in the media. It also means not harming other creatures that live on this planet and taking care of the environment we live in.

Ahimsa affected my thoughts on drinking because it asks us to look at the harm we are doing to ourselves. By drinking and smoking I knew I was harming myself, but thinking about Ahimsa really made me contemplate it at a deeper level. I made efforts to stop being so cruelly judgemental to myself as well as to others. I reflected on the harm that my drinking habits were doing to others, especially my children. On its own wasn't enough to change my behaviour, after all I had known that my behaviour was harmful for years, but this self-study was part of a bigger and more profound process.

*Satya*

Satya means truthfulness. At the most basic level it means that you shouldn't tell lies. In his 'The Lost Teachings of Yoga', Georg Fuerstein tells us there are 6 types of lie: -

The blatant lie

The white lie

Lying by silence

Advertising

Statistics

Politics

While this made me laugh the first time I heard it, there is so much truth in it. I would add a 7th lie of 'media' as I think we all know our media sources are highly biased and not above blatantly making up stories to affect the mindset of their readers.

Beyond not lying to others, Satya tells us we should not lie to ourselves. This is really hard to change, as most of us probably don't realise just how much we do it. We procrastinate on work that needs to be done telling ourselves we'll 'do it tomorrow', we think we are either much better or much worse at something than we actually are and we have often an inflated or reduced sense of our own value. Our ideas of truth are always based on our perceptions of events as oppose to reality. Similarly, our memories of events are far from factual records as they are affected by both our perceptions at the time, and how we perceive the event from the time we are remembering it.

Satya also teaches us to be true to who we are, to learn to see past the walls, the barriers and the filters we put up around ourselves to shield us from ourselves and our world; to see the real Self inside. For years I had an idea of myself I called 'fantasy Esther', she was everything I wanted to be but didn't think I ever could be. Once I started to really understand yoga, I realised I was starting to become her. Fantasy Esther wasn't a fantasy at all, but the true Me. I am still not there yet, but am getting closer to her all the time.

• • •

When we are living in accordance with Satya, our values, our inner barometer of who and how we should be, it shows in our behaviour and we can start to feel more at ease with ourselves.

When I was drinking, although I dreamed about 'Fantasy Esther', I fought any desire to actually become her. I completely identified with this idea of myself as a frantic drunk, even though I would never admit to myself the truth that I was an alcoholic. I wouldn't allow the true Me to surface at all. The minute I started to hear that voice, the one that reminded me I wanted happiness, not wine, I would reach for another glass, or another cigarette, and push it away. Eventually, through the yoga practices I was learning, I was able to break down the barriers I had built and started to want to get to know the real me more. I realised I needed to be OK with the pain and the unhappiness I had been hiding from, to face it so that I could start to heal it. Once I began to do this, it became easy for me to release myself from the grip of alcoholism.

*Asteya*

Asteya is non-stealing. It is obvious, of course that this means that we should not steal from others and most of us wouldn't think twice about doing so. Or would we? Do you download from torrent sites on the internet? Many people do this and don't think consider it stealing but it's not any different to walking into a shop and putting a CD in your pocket. I used to do this all the time and thought nothing of it. Eventually the lessons of Asteya filtered through to me and I no longer download any album or film without paying for it.

There are many ways we can steal from others without taking their property. We can take someone's time, demanding their attention when it is really needed elsewhere. We may take credit for someone else's work, borrow things and never return them or steal someone's ideas and claim them for our own.

Through contemplation of Asteya I came to realise I was very guilty of this in many ways. I was particularly struck by how much I was taking from my children; I would often steal their time especially when I spent many weekends and holidays hung over. I would sometimes rush through bedtime stories or omit them completely so that I could go to my wine downstairs. If I was drinking with friends I would often put listening to them above listening to the children. What was even more damaging though was how I was denying them a healthy life, a healthy view of themselves and of the world by putting my negativity and addiction in the way of my parenting. I was making it very likely that Marcus would have to deal with losing his mother through alcohol related illness at a young age. I was 37 when he was born, so was already an 'old' Mum, I need to do everything I can to ensure I live as long as possible for his sake. I was doing the exact opposite of this and also increasing the likelihood that my parents would have to say goodbye to another child, something I know would cause my mother in particular no end of pain and grief. I never wanted to do that to her, but was unable to stop my drinking despite knowing that I was putting my life at risk every time I did it.

I also started to see how much I was taking from myself through my addiction. I was denying myself the opportunity to grow and learn from life's experiences. By drinking to escape my emotions rather than exploring them I was missing out. I was also stopping myself from doing other, more life affirming, and beneficial activities.

Swami Gitananda tells us that procrastination is theft. This is one of my biggest weaknesses nowadays. I have been exploring this a lot recently, and have come to the conclusion that I am addicted to procrastination. Steven Pressfield, in The War of Art, tells us that procrastination is a device of resistance, and that 'what we resist most is what we most need for our soul's growth'. How ironic is this, the things we most need to do in order to grow are the things we find ourselves most resistant to. Swami Gitananda calls this 'wasting the time of the Spirit', and tells us this is theft. This he would consider the worst theft of all, as the purpose of life is to evolve and grow on a spiritual level. I certainly know I am far more content in life if I do the things I need to do, such as write this book, than if I flitter my day away avoiding the task.

*Brahmacharya*

This Yama is often translated as celibacy. While it needn't mean absolute celibacy, it does mean behaving with restraint and not succumbing to every physical desire of the body. It can be applied to many areas of life. In the devout Yogi, it would mean complete abstinence from any form of sexual activity or sexual thought but it is possible to bring this Yama into life without this extreme interpretation. Georg Fuerstein advises us that complete abstinence is not for everyone, and that one shouldn't feel bad if it is not possible. It is better to aim for moderation of behaviour and succeed at it than aim for abstinence and spend our whole life anxious of failure. I would never try to commit to this fully. While sex is not a big issue to me now, I do not want to rule it out completely for the rest of my life! Devout Yogis would reserve sexual activity only for the purposes of procreation in marriage. I am unmarried and certainly don't want any more children. However, younger, more insecure Esther would have benefitted from thinking about Brahmacharya a little, as it might have helped her to see that casual sex was no substitute for love and self-esteem. Just because men wanted to sleep with her, it didn't mean that she had to let them.

Swami Gitananda, in his Step by Step course, tells us that there are other interpretations of this Yama. Brahmacharya refers to not allowing things that over stimulate the senses and emotions into our life. In our modern world this can also refer to violent films, loud music and a desire for possessions and over indulgent foods. It means not allowing desires and addictions to control our lives and behaviour, it means learning to control the impulses and constant desire for sensory pleasure and to master self-control. It teaches delayed or denied gratification, a skill we are in danger of losing completely in our 'have it NOW' society. It helps us to remember that just because we think we want something, it doesn't mean we have to have it. We often find that when we succumb to such urges, the object of desire ends up being disappointing. Anyone who has experienced 'buyer's remorse' will testify to this.

I imagine that modern Yoga scholars will also cite use of the internet as something that needs to be controlled through Brahmacharya. In the age of smart phones and social media, internet addiction is becoming increasingly problematic, making us incredibly overstimulated and constantly seeking stimulus. Brahmacharya may be the hardest Yama for modern western Yoga practitioners to master as our society is engineered to make us want possessions and constant sensory stimulation. It takes a great deal of effort to break the patterning that tells us that material possessions bring happiness, that sex is vital for self-esteem and happiness and that alcohol is the best way to relax and socialise. I certainly have succumbed to this idea many times and have sought happiness, self-worth and fulfilment in sensory experiences. I am sure I will again (the pleasure to be found in dark chocolate can be incredibly seductive), but I try to limit the times I succumb, and am mindful of moments when succumbing to my desires would actually result in me feeling worse about myself than I did beforehand.

*Aparigraha*

This is closely related to Brahmarachya in that it tells us not to take more than we are entitled to, not to hoard possessions, not to be selfish or greedy and not to exploit others. It can also be applied to people in our lives. We shouldn't make unreasonable demands on people or try to 'possess' them. We shouldn't seek happiness in material possessions or others. We find can only find true happiness through our own spiritual development.

Addiction makes us selfish and greedy. We don't choose to be, but it is the nature of the beast – we place more importance on acquiring the object of our addiction than we do on other things. Life revolves around the addiction. For some this means spending the day doing anything required to enable them to get the next fix. For others it means getting through the 'normal' day so that you can shut the door on the world and cocoon yourself in your addiction. I would prioritise my need for alcohol and cigarettes above pretty much everything else. I would feed the children, they never went hungry and I had a rule that unless we were socialising with friends, I didn't start drinking until they were in bed. I would construct reasons to have company, either inviting people around or visiting. I don't want any friends reading this to think that my friendship was false, I did enjoy their company, but often the main driver was having 'an excuse' to drink or not wanting to drink alone. I allowed friends to buy my drinks and cigarettes, as my desired consumption often far exceeded my available funds, and was not averse to sneakily taking mouthfuls of their drinks when they went to the loo. So while I was never going out and actively stealing to get my fix, I was taking what wasn't freely given and exploiting the good nature of my friends. Thinking about trying to live more in line with Aparigraha meant that I felt a greater need to contribute and 'pay my way'.

This need to ensure that we contribute seems to be a very common theme in addiction recovery. The addiction sector seems to be run largely by volunteers and staff who are themselves in recovery. It seems that after a lifetime of taking and grasping in order to feed the addiction monster, former addicts see the massive value in giving back to their communities. In my experience it feels good to contribute to the services that supported my recovery and to help others in the same situation. I feel a lot better about my past knowing that I can take what I have learned from my addiction and misery and put it to good use through writing this book, and sharing my knowledge through classes and workshops. I have attended a couple of conferences and events which showcase the huge amount of contribution ex and current services users make to the addiction recovery sector. Many organisations wouldn't function without them, it is truly heartening to see. In my view, it also utterly negates the judgemental view society makes that addicts are 'bad people'. If they were bad people, they would be such with or without their addiction.

This act of helping others may help to develop the empathy that the addicted brain shuts down. Research suggests that rather than fostering feelings of pleasure in individuals, acts of altruism actually develop the posterior superior temporal cortex, the part of the brain that is concerned with the feelings of others. (Tankersley et al, Altruism is associated with an increased neural response to Agency, 2007).

## Niyamas

If the Yamas tell us what we shouldn't be doing with our bodies and minds, the Niyamas tell us what we should be doing to enhance ourselves and become the very best versions of ourselves. The Niyamas help us with our spiritual growth, and help us reach our potential, both in the material world and in our spiritual life.

## Saucha

This Niyama refers to purity and cleanliness of the body, mind and emotions. It tells us that we should take care of personal hygiene and wear clean clothes, but it goes far deeper than that. It refers to internal cleanliness, so we should take care that what we put into our bodies is clean, nutritious and not harmful. Saucha reminds us that our thoughts, words and actions need to be wholesome. This would include stopping negative emotions from taking control of us. It encourages us to free ourselves of preconceived notions and prejudices and to have an open mind to the ideas and opinions of others, even those we disagree with; a fresh approach to an issue can lead to new solutions to problems.

Saucha also refers to our external environment and encourages us to keep our living space clean. We need to pay heed to the needs of the wider environment and live in a sustainable life that doesn't harm the natural world around us.

Sacha encourages us to live a simple life with little clutter, both in our environment and in ourselves. Anyone who has ever had a clear out in their home will recognise that the process seems to clear the mind as well. This is because you're freeing up mental as well as physical space.

Although thinking about Saucha didn't tell me anything I didn't already know about what I was doing to my body and mind by drinking and smoking, my desire to live according to the values of Yoga did meant that I was at last forced to contemplate this on a different level. It stopped being about avoiding harm and became about becoming healthy which is a very different perspective. In NLP terms this is about having a 'toward' rather than an 'away from' mindset. Focussing on the positives I could gain was far more motivating than the fear of what I was risking.

Drinking was clearly harming my body, but it was also doing the same to my mind; the thought patterns that led me to the off licence and the thoughts I would have when drunk were damaging to myself. I developed quite a nasty sense of humour and was a horrible and careless neighbour, playing loud music late at night with no regard for others. I would prioritise drinking over personal or domestic hygiene and the rubbish I would generate in was harming the environment, despite my outward claims to care about environmental issues! Physically, a drinking session would involve chain smoking while remaining stationary. Nothing in my life was clean.

### Santosha

Santosha is the mental calm that comes as the result of a calm and peaceful mind. This sense of calm allows us to forge deeper, more meaningful relationships with others. When our mind in constantly busy it does not have space for this level of spiritual or personal intimacy. Santosha allows us to find constant peace and contentment within ourselves instead of needing to find it in things that are external to ourselves. Conditions cannot destroy our contentment when we are living in Santosha. Yoga tells us that one of the root causes of unhappiness is desire. If we can be content in our current lives, we can eliminate this desire and find inner peace.

## Santosha and Gratitude

How we view the world very much shapes our experience of it. If we are always expecting negative things to happen, if we always focus on what we don't have rather than what we do have, then we are going to experience unhappiness. Santosha teaches us to be satisfied and content with what we have, to be grateful for what is good in our life and to look for the positives. This is such a powerful practice, and something that certainly helps me in my sobriety. Santosha reminds us that while we may have troubles in life and we may not have all that we want or even need but we do still have blessings. If we focus on those, then we will feel a level of contentment that is impossible if we are constantly worrying about what is missing from our life.

Much has been written on the benefits of a gratitude practice. It has been reported to improve physical and mental health, increase mental resilience, empathy and self-esteem. It promotes better sleep and reduces aggression[3]. All of these benefits are very important to the recovery process; they create resilience and personal recovery capital and are a crucial set of inner resources that are needed for sustainable recovery. Practicing gratitude supports recovery from mental illness as well as addiction and in fact is beneficial to everyone. If we ensure that we have these inner resources, we may well be able to avoid mental illness and addiction in the first place.

---

[3] http://www.forbes.com/sites/amymorin/2014/11/23/7-scientifically-proven-benefits-of-gratitude-that-will-motivate-you-to-give-thanks-year-round/#38c4f9aa6800

## Tapas

The literal translation of Tapas is fire. It refers to the fire of discipline and personal control. Tapas tells us that we must be disciplined in our practice and in our day to day life. It requires focus, dedication and commitment to our goals. It means that we approach our Yoga practice with the 3 R's of Yoga – Repetition, Regularity and Rhythm.

A half-hearted, sporadic effort at a Yoga practice is not going to yield much reward compared to a regular and dedicated routine. Similarly, Tapas applies in our life away from the Yoga mat, we should approach all our work in the same manner. For example, I want to write this book. In order to do this, I must write regularly, with dedication and with focus – I will never write a book if I only write 20 words a day, writing when I feel like it. I am making myself write every day until this writing is finished. I will continue to write on a daily basis once this is done because I recognise that it is of great benefit me in my Swadhyaya.

Tapas helped me in my recovery because it created a mindset shift that was vital if I was ever to be free. I look back in horror now at the many occasions when I would leave a Yoga class, full of self-righteous feelings of 'being good' because I had 'done Yoga', then proceed to open a bottle of wine, roll a joint and ended the night in familiar oblivion. I had no idea then that Yoga was so much more than the exercise class I was attending and saw no contradiction in my behaviour. It was only when I saw that personal self-control and discipline were a crucial aspect of Yoga that I began to free myself from my addiction and self-destruction. Patanjali tells us that "the fire of discipline destroys all impurities, resulting in mastery of body and senses".

My brother got married about 6 weeks after my alcoholic revelation, I had decided that I wasn't going to drink at all that day despite the proliferation of good quality red wine and champagne that was going to be available on request throughout the day. Although I had told my family that I was not going to be drinking, I don't think anyone would have objected much if I had. I did stick to my resolution and the realisation that I was able to enjoy myself, look after Marcus and not do anything to embarrass myself or my family was wonderful. I enjoyed waking up the following day with no feelings of shame or discomfort, feeling happy, awake and full of energy. It was that day I realised I had definitely given up drinking, and the first time I felt sure that being an ex-drinker was my new identity.

## Swadhyaya

Swadhyaya is 'introspectional self-analysis', or self-study. The ultimate aim of it in Yoga is to help us to connect with the Divine aspect of us. Before we can get to that stage of Self-knowledge, we must first learn who we are in this life, why we have the life we have and how we can make sure we learn the lessons this life has to offer us.

This is a very important and incredibly useful practice to incorporate into life. It is impossible to make meaningful change in life without first looking at where we are and trying to understand why. Bringing awareness to our life through our thoughts, words and actions is a crucial first step to breaking bad habits, and creating new, healthier habits.

I spent much of my adult life actively avoiding looking too closely at myself. When I did look, I always saw faults that I didn't want to admit to, features that I didn't like, and behaviours I was ashamed of. Instead of trying to change, I would try to hide my mistakes and find someone or something to blame. I would quickly become very defensive or alternatively I would become dismissive of my failings. I rarely admitted I was wrong or apologised.

Yoga teacher training forced me to look very closely at myself and I am so grateful for this. While I was utterly unable to stick to keeping the diary we were supposed to keep (a valuable topic of self-analysis in itself!) my answers to the essay questions posed to us elicited a great of self-study. By exploring the philosophy and practices I was learning about and applying them to my life, I was able to discover truths, thoughts and patterns of behaviour in myself I had never been aware of before. I enjoyed the free flowing writing element as I allowed my subconscious mind to direct me. Many times I found myself staring in amazement at something I had just written, astonished at the revelation that had come to me without my conscious mind being aware!

It was through this practice that I realised how hugely beneficial writing was. I learned a great deal about myself and I finally faced some painful truths. I did so for the first time with honestly and with gratitude. Every painful realisation became an opportunity to grow, to lay demons to rest, to become more aware and to change the parts of me that really didn't fit anymore.

Awareness is more than mere intellectual awareness. I was aware before I smoked my first joint that drugs can be harmful. I knew very well the destructive nature of alcohol as one of my earliest memories is of being terrified by my Nana in a drunken rage, and I certainly knew that smoking was bad - my brother and I had even terrorised our father into giving up when we were small. I didn't start doing any of these things because I didn't know they were bad for me. On some level that was probably part of the appeal, they suited my self-destructive need for oblivion. The awareness I got from my Swadhyaya helped me to quit because I reflected on the origins of this self-destructive drive in me, and still do. Whenever I notice a pattern of behaviour I don't like, I ask myself, "Where does this come from?"

An important part of Swadhyaya is that you must observe yourself without judgement. This does not come easy, as we are steeped in fixed ideas of good and bad. When we learn to step away from this habit and just see things as facts, we can look more objectively at events without passing value judgements or trying to second guess motives.

While Swadhyaya can help us to see that events and actions in the past have lead us to where we are today, it is important that we don't blame the past, and that we don't spend too much time focusing on it. In 'Understanding the Yoga Darshan, Dr Ananda says:

*"Today will be the past tomorrow, and tomorrow will soon be today. So make use of the present moment for it is only in the present that one may change the future"*

Swadhyaya helped me to see that I have complete responsibility for my life, my emotions and my happiness. Whatever has happened in my past has happened, and I can choose to dwell on the negative aspects of those events, or to find the lessons to be learned. Looking slightly more objectively at my past experiences has helped me develop compassion towards myself and to others. I can now see that my past actions have been the result of patterns of behaviour that developed in me as a result of my perception. This perception has nothing to do with other people, and everything to do with me. Most of these perceptions began to be formed when I was a very small child. That small child could only make sense of the world from a very narrow perspective, but that perspective led me to make many conclusions about the world, and my place in it. I carried these with me into adulthood. It is only through my Swadhyaya that I have been able to see the conclusions I formed as a child, and the patterns of self-destructive behaviour that flowed from them. Armed with this knowledge, I have been able to break many of these patterns to create a far happier, healthier present and future.

I still practice Swadhyaya on a regular basis. This book is, essentially, an exercise in Swadhyaya, I am learning a great deal about myself while writing this, not least of all how I struggle to deal with resistance to writing. Steven Pressfield, in 'The War of Art' tells us that the things we feel the greatest resistance to are the things we most need for our spiritual growth. I can identify with this so much – my greatest resistances in life come from the things I actually most want to do in order to make my life better!

Through this work I do I am able to get closer and closer to the true me, the me that is timeless, fearless, joyful and at peace. It is impossible to get to this true self through denial and oblivion seeking. Swadhyaya helped me get sober and my continued sobriety helps me in my Swadhyaya.

## Ishwara Pranidhana

Ishwara Pranidhana, or, as Swami Gitananda called it, Atman Pranidhana, is surrender to a higher power than ourselves. It is acceptance that we are bound to a bigger Self than our individual egos, souls and bodies. People often say things like 'God moves in mysterious ways', or 'things happen for a reason' which reveals some degree of this surrender. Asmita, the Klesha of egoism, makes this acceptance difficult, which is why we need to work to rise above the Kleshas. We often don't like to accept that we cannot control everything, and this leads to much unhappiness. Relinquishing control can feel like failure, but it is really the ultimate in liberation.

That is not to say that we don't have our role to play, that we should just shrug our shoulder and do nothing. Ishwara Pranidhana reminds us that we cannot ever really create the end result; we can only take the required action with the best effort and accept the consequences as they come. As Swamiji used to say 'do your best and leave the rest', the universe will take care of the results. Often the results that we want are not the results that we get. This can lead to stress and upset if we are overly attached to the results, but if we surrender we can be happy that we get the results that are meant to be.

I am currently experiencing a need to surrender during the process of writing this book. I am finding that I am not writing the book I had thought I was going to write. For a while I fought this, thinking that if I couldn't write the book I wanted to write, I may as well not write a book at all, but eventually I realised that I can write the book that is being written now.

I have no control over the outcome of my work; all I can control is the effort I put into writing the book. I can control the words I write and I can control my decision to publish it. Beyond that, it is not in my hands. I cannot control what anyone else thinks of it, I cannot control the impact, if any, that it will have in other people's lives. All I know for sure is that I must write it, my soul has been calling out for me to and if I don't, I don't think I will ever feel happy. While I sincerely hope it touches you on some level, to a very large extent that is not part of my journey, once you have it, it is out of my hands.

When we plant a seed and nurture that seed until it bears fruit, we may congratulate ourselves on our good gardening skills, but the best gardener in the world cannot grow a seed to a fruit alone. The traditional practice of celebrating the harvest is a form of accepting the surrender to a higher consciousness. When we say grace before food, or thank 'God', this is another example of surrender.

This is one of the main premises behind the Alcoholics Anonymous philosophy; we need to accept that a force greater than our selves can help us. This is off putting to many as it conjures up images of a God which may not have significance in our lives. As I have already discussed in a previous chapter, I had scant regard for a God that I felt was both meaningless and destructive in my life; there was no way I was going to put my faith in *that* god for help. When I learned that Yoga was a way to connect deeply to myself, and that I could take responsibility for my own recovery, I realised recovery was a possibility. While I accepted, at last, full responsibility for my life and my recovery, I knew that I was not embarking on the journey alone. There was a very definite acceptance of a higher power into my life, but it was a recognition that the higher power exists as *my* personal power and my connection to it. I may not have a name for this Higher Power, but I know it is there. That is all I need to know.

Swami Gitananda calls Ishwara Pranidhana 'Atman Pranidhana'. Atman is the Sanskrit word which refers to the Self, the true essence of who we are. So Swamiji is telling us that Atman Pranidhana is not listening to 'God' but having the courage to listen to our own inner wisdom. This can be incredibly hard; often our inner wisdom is telling us things that the ego really doesn't want to listen to. Think of the angel and devil on the shoulders of cartoon characters, the inner wisdom and the ego in conflict, which does the character usually listen to? If we stop, listen and act on our inner wisdom, we will rarely go wrong. For many of us, it can be hard to even hear our inner wisdom, Yoga helps us to develop our ability to listen to, and trust ourselves.

In the activity pack I have created to accompany this book there is a video in which I talk through a technique to still the mind and find peace. This is what many people call meditation, through regular practice of this technique, you may find that you can learn to hear and trust your inner wisdom. You can access this pack by visiting http://bit.ly/bent_shape.

# Asana – so much more than touching toes

When we in the West think of Yoga, we tend to think of the body. Yoga to us is an exercise system which improves flexibility, we think of the 'pretzel' type postures which seem utterly inaccessible to most of us. Many people think that if they aren't flexible, then they can't 'do' yoga. The West, unfortunately, has largely missed the point. Yoga was never meant to be a fitness craze. Asana, the part of Yoga that is related to the body, is just one part of Yoga.

Patanjali's Yoga Sutras is the definitive guide Yoga. Modern Yoga practitioners would probably be surprised to discover that Asana is only mentioned four times in the whole of this text, and even more surprised to learn that at no time is a single physical posture referred to.

At the time of Patanjali, yoga was the preserve of the ascetic, the devout men who devoted their whole life to spiritual practice, to experimentation, solitary living and meditative practices. For these men, the only asana necessary was the ability to sit still for extended periods in order to be able to enter deep meditative states. Asana originates from the word asi, which means to sit. Asana refers to a firm seat. In the Bhagavad Gita, we learn its original meaning, when Krishna uses the term to mean the mat that should be used to sit on.

In the modern world, we need the physical postures we now call Asanas in order to make our body fit and able to sit in meditative postures for long periods of time. Without developing flexibility, strength and stamina in the body we would not be able to become absorbed in breath because we would be too focussed on the discomfort in the body. Western lifestyles are now very sedentary. We spend far too much of our time sitting in chairs, and adopt unnatural postures.

Through practice of Asanas we are able to release physical tension in the body that could otherwise cause us to feel stress. Many of the postures we practice in Gitananda Yoga have numerous benefits for the mind and body as they stimulate and relax systems as well as tone the muscles and joints, promoting flexibility. Yoga is well known to be good for warding off the symptoms of aging but did you know that Yoga can affect the body at a cellular level? It promotes healing and recovery in all cells in the body. When you look at older Yoga practitioners, you will normally see a vitality in them that defies their age. This is the effect their practice has on every aspect of their being.

Yoga asana can be of tremendous benefit in recovery from addiction. As well as the obvious boost to physical fitness and flexibility, which can be needed after extended periods of substance abuse, asanas bring fitness and flexibility to the mind as well. Asanas can bring stillness and peace where we feel noise and restlessness. They promote strength when we feel weak, flexibility when we feel tense and clarity when we feel scattered. It brings about a sense of wellbeing and achievement when we feel worthless and hopeless. Through learning to be still in a posture, even if only for a few seconds at a time, we learn to delay gratification and not to give up when something is hard

As part of the bonus pack that I am offering with this book, there are videos and photographs of practices and postures, and relaxation mp3s available. Further details are available at http://bit.ly/bent_shape.

# Relaxation

The postures that have been developed over the years are now necessary to create healthy bodies, but it is important to remember they are not the main point of Yoga. Before I discovered Gitananda Yoga, I would go to yoga classes, enjoy the postures, and put up with the breath work. I didn't fully relax and would return to my stressful, alcohol dependant life straight away. Yoga has to be understood as something more than what happens in the yoga class.

It has since been pointed out that maybe, far from helping me to relax and reduce my stress, the Yoga I was doing back in my addicted days may have actually been making the situation worse. I was putting lots of tension into my body while I practiced the asanas, and never properly relaxed or allowed the tension to dissipate. While the asanas in a yoga class are very good for the mental and physical health, they are only as good as the relaxation that follows them.

Gitananda Yoga places a great deal of emphasis on teaching the body and mind the difference between tension and relaxation, a practice known as Loma Viloma, or tension/non tension. After each posture that creates tension in the body, we spend a few moments allowing the body to rest, bringing the breath and heart rate back to normal and letting the muscles relax. This seems odd when you first do it as part of a class, but in time you start to notice subtle changes in your stress response as your body starts to recognise the things that put stress on your body. I started to realise very early on in my training that things that used to really wind me up suddenly didn't bother me.

I noticed it first when driving. I used to drive in a near permanent state of road rage. Within a very short space of time, I became a much calmer and I even started to enjoy driving.

This ability to moderate the stress response is crucial to ability to take control of an addiction or even just to be able to gain connection with our self. We often use our addiction to numb our emotions and allow us to be able to 'relax'. When we try to remove that crutch we use to lean on, relaxation can be very difficult and we can find ourselves feeling even more stressed than usual, creating a vicious circle of need. If we can train the mind and body to relax in a way that we are in control of then these stress related complications will be lessened in recovery.

Yoga offers a deep, four-fold approach to relaxation. It is not something you should expect to be able to 'do' straight away, but practice of the techniques I am giving you should help you to achieve greater relaxation over time.

In this part of the book, I invite to think about how you can apply these to your life. What barriers can you let down, what stress can you release and how can you give in to your Inner Self?

## Letting Down

This does not mean 'letting ourselves or others down' as we understand the term. It is to do with the barriers we put up between ourselves and the world. These barriers stop you from hearing advice or accepting help. The preconceived ideas you have about the world that creates judgement and prejudices can often mean we are missing out on beneficial new experiences. It means to let down the ideas that we are conditioned into by society for example, we MUST be beautiful, we MUST be successful and such like.

**What barriers do you have that aren't serving you? Can you start to take them down?**

## Giving Up

This does not relate to the giving up on a goal. I gave up alcohol, but in order to do that I had to give up and let go of a lot emotionally before I could succeed.

We carry around so much stress in our everyday life. It is almost a trophy; people compete to be the hardest working or the most committed. Our culture seems to encourage us to be stressed. But we don't have to be. We CAN give up the modern addiction of being stressed. Stress and tension beyond that needed for survival create ill health and unhappiness; it serves no one apart from the industries that make millions from it.

**What are you stressed out about right now? Write it all down, journal it, see what comes up for you when you do this.**

**Practice the 'throwing out' exercise provided in the bonus pack that accompanies this book whenever you find yourself getting stressed, practice it in the morning so you can start your day with less tension, or at bedtime to relax your body (the bonus pack can be accessed by visiting http://bit.ly/bent_shape**

**Use the relaxation MP3 I have provided in the pack to help you to deeply relax your body and mind when you are able to take 15 minutes to relax, it doesn't only need to be done at the end of your breathing course practice.**

## Giving In

This, to my interpretation, is about finding what ignites your soul, and giving in to this. The Inner Self is our spiritual aspect, one which many of us don't understand the importance of. We can only be truly happy when the mind, body and spirit are all in harmony. Soul is not about religion, but I know my soul sings when I am in nature, in particular when I am near trees. This creates deep relaxation and joy inside of me.

**What can you give in to that relaxes and soothes your Inner Self, your soul? Do you do this often enough? Could you do it more?**

## Giving Over

This is Ishwara Pranidhana, the Niyama discussed in the last chapter. It involves giving over control to the Divine, to Fate, to the Universe, to chance or whatever term you want to apply to it. It is about letting go of trying to control the outcomes. We can only control our actions; we cannot control the end result and we cannot control others'.

Attempts to control outcomes often lead to disappointment and feelings of failure. When we are trying to control others, it can lead to resentment and frustration on both sides.

We should not give up responsibility and simply 'put things in God's hand' by any means, instead we must take full ownership of our life and the impact we have on others, it is simply about recognising that we cannot control every aspect of life.

**Where can you try to give over a little more, let go of control? If you are very control oriented this will need to be in small steps. Don't try to let go of everything or you will feel very uncomfortable. Think of an area of your life where you can let go a little and see how it evolves.**

**It is important to remember that this is not an 'overnight success' process, it is a journey. Take these steps a little at a time, and be kind to yourself – don't expect to immediately 'get it' or to immediately be able to 'do it'. Don't allow thoughts of failure to infiltrate your mind, there is no such thing as failure as long as you are making the effort. Yoga is very allowing and rewards effort, but over time, it is not a quick fix.**

# Stress reduction through a Yoga class

The structure of a Gitananda general Yoga class is geared towards stress reduction. From start to finish, the student is encouraged to release tension from the body and mind. Most classes in the Gitananda tradition follow the same structure, a structure that has been based on ancient wisdom about the best way to induce relaxation in the mind and body.

At the start of the class we sit quietly observing the breath for a few minutes. This is a gentle form of Pratyahara, concentration. It is very hard to retain the focus on the breath, and the training teaches you how to recognise your mind once it has wandered so you can pull it back to the breath. This practice can be used in everyday life; when negative thoughts infect our mind we can focus on our breathing to dissolve them. This 'quiet sitting' gives us the opportunity to put aside the worries of the day and prepare ourselves for Yoga. If we are able to do this, we may find that when we go to 'pick them up again' after class, the worries are no longer there or are no longer so heavy!

Coming from the quiet sitting with an 'Om' and chanting the Guru Gayatri reminds us that we are not alone, we are part of the greater universal consciousness. This helps us to connect with the higher force and enables us to 'give in' to the Higher Consciousness and begin to be at one with the Universe. This process reduces our focus on our external worries and stress.

In our general class, we then practice Jattis. These gentle, simple movements can seem strange to Western students used to going straight into a dynamic class, but they are, to my mind, some of the best minutes of the class. Jattis gets the body loose and ready for the postures, it releases tension and toxins from the body, increases blood flow around the body and increases flexibility in the joints. As we store so much of our tension in our joints, this practice really is invaluable. I have found that simply practicing Jattis followed by relaxation can lead to a great sense of relaxation. Ammaji has said that the Jattis offers such sufficient health benefits even if it was practiced alone.

Following the Jattis we do our breathing practices. These include the Shasha Asanas, Pranava Aum, or Vibhaga Pranayama. This ensures that our body and mind are relaxed and that we have a good supply of oxygen to perform the postures to come. It is important that we move from sitting to standing and back again slowly to avoid disturbing the nervous system. We move up by first coming into Meru Asana, then slowly moving to standing before practicing some standing jattis.

The practice of 'throwing out' that we do at the end of the Jattis is a great stress reliever, and one that can be helpful as a tool to take into daily life. It really focuses the mind on the process of releasing tension, both physical and mental. As we throw out and then relax the body, we can really feel the tension releasing through the arms, I like to focus my students' attention on this release. One of my students uses this technique frequently in work and tells me that it has made a huge difference to how she feels through her working day, even just knowing that she has this tool at her disposal has relaxes her.

We then practice a variation of Surya Namaskar, offering great benefits to the cardio vascular system, this gets the blood flowing and is particularly helpful after our deep breathing because the blood pumped is well oxygenated. Surya Namaskar helps almost every part of the body, improving bodily functions and improving flexibility and posture, all of which helps the mind to remain more relaxed. Following the Surya Namaskar we rest the body, allowing it to become aware of the difference between tension and relaxation. In the process of doing this we slow the breath, ensuring that both mind and body are calm before beginning the next postures.

We then practice some standing postures and balances. Both of these groups are very beneficial for mental health conditions. The standing postures increase body awareness, which we know becomes decreased when the mind is stressed or unhealthy. Both the general standing postures and the balances promote focus and concentration, this is particularly challenging for the stressed mind, so anything that allows even a few seconds of focus helps the healing process.

Following the standing postures, we come back to the floor, again. We do this slowly and carefully to avoid putting undue stress on the nervous system. Once here we do some seated postures. Often these will be leg lifting, taking elements from the Loma Viloma series of postures. These postures strengthen the core muscles and create a central store of energy that we can turn to when we feel depleted.

From these postures we then come into relaxation. The relaxation following an hour and a half class needs to be at least 10 minutes as the body and mind need this to get the full benefits of the relaxation. A variety of relaxation techniques can be used and it depends on the work that has been done throughout the session and the level of experience the students have.

Our class ends with the Shanti Mantra, a wish for peace and wellbeing for every being on the planet. This serves to remind us of our connectedness with the world and the universe. It reminds us that we are not alone.

Videos and photographs demonstrating the postures and practices named above, and others, can be found in the bonus pack that comes with this book, details can be found at http://bit.ly/bent_shape.

# Pranayama

While Yoga has many routes to help clear and quieten the mind, the main tool that we use is the breath.

Breath is vital to life. It is the first thing we do when we enter the world, and the last thing we do when we leave. At its most basic level it provides the body with oxygen and eliminates waste products from respiration.

Our breath is an automatic function carried out by our brain but we can take it under our conscious control. When we do this, we breathe better, we gain a greater sense of calm and control and we develop the ability to focus the mind and quieten the noise that keeps us so distracted.

The breath is also the way in which we get Prana into the body. Prana is so much more than breath. It is a source of energy, a vital life force. Pranayama is the means by which we control the intake and release of Prana.

Pranayama is a vital part of the yogic journey. Patanjali tells us that no one can possibly hope to achieve the later limbs of Pratyahara, Dharana, Dhyana and Samadhi without having first mastered the fourth limb of Pranayama. Patanjali believed that it was vital to master the first 3 limbs of Yama, Niyama and Asana before Pranayama can be mastered, although I learned about them concurrently and it certainly had positive effects on me.

Pranayama offers tremendous physical, mental and emotional benefits to the body and mind, bringing greater health to almost all aspects of the human life. Pranayama allows the mind to quieten and calms the emotions. The Four Fold Awareness of Yoga teaches us that the emotions have a direct effect on the body, and that the mind can affect the emotions. So by simply calming the mind and the emotions, Pranayama can influence the health of the body as well as the mind. Pranayama can do so much more.

Pranayama can increase muscle strength, circulation, lung function, metabolism, brain function, altitude tolerance and relaxation. The body functions better because Pranayama involves breathing with the whole lung, rather than the shallower breathing that is more common. Shallow breathing can cause or exacerbate many physical health problems, as the body doesn't receive the amount of oxygen it needs to fully nourish the cells.

Through Pranayama, the blood pressure drops and the lungs get a full workout; the body gets all the oxygen it needs, and rids itself of more carbon dioxide. This means that every cell in the body can work better and is in greater balance. Pranayama can balance the nervous system, taking us from the sympathetic nervous system and its flight or fight response towards the control of the parasympathetic nervous system, the calm, peaceful rest and digest response.

At its most basic physiological level, Pranayama involves deeper, longer inhalation and exhalation than the unconscious breath we usually take. Therefore, the lungs are receiving more oxygen with each inhalation, and removing more carbon dioxide with every exhalation. This gaseous exchange is vital for the healthy functioning of all cells in the body, taking in more oxygen and releasing more carbon dioxide will immediately have a positive effect on each and every cell in the body.

However, Prana is so much more than oxygen. It is Universal Energy, the timeless life force that connects us with the universe. Prana has been stated to be 'the fundamental basis of whatever is, was and will be', so by connecting with Prana through our Pranayama, we are connecting with something eternal and ancient that unites all life. You could call this God, Divine, self, Atma, nature, universe, or anything else that works as a concept for you.

The mind is allowed to still during Pranayama, allowing the quietening of the 'monkey mind' and a great sense of clarity. In the second Sutra, Maharishi Patanjali tells us;

*Yoga is the cessation of the whirlpools of the subconscious mind.*

Through the practice of Yoga, and by adopting its teachings into our life, we can learn to control the mind, to find calm and stillness, and to quieten the noise in our minds.

This noise can be the source of much anxiety. It can keep us awake at night; stop us from being able to focus on the task in hand, from being able to move on from a particular thought or emotion. It can be, as it is for many, a reason to seek out a way to 'numb' ourselves, to seek a way to be able to block out the noise. For me, it was one of the reasons I turned to drink, as drinking enabled me to "sleep" at night, rather than listen to the thoughts that would revolve around my mind when I got into bed, and to 'be with myself'.

While the benefits of Pranayama would lead to an overall healthier, more energetic, better functioning body and mind in anyone, it is particularly beneficial for the recovery process, as it helps to combat all the unpleasant side effects of withdrawal. It brings the body and mind into balance and helps the development of coping techniques that create the much needed resilience or personal recovery capital.

## Quiet Sitting

Every class I teach begins with 'quiet sitting'. This is a practice not unlike the "mindfulness meditation" practiced by so many. This is a very simple way to gain some stillness in the mind, and to "turn off the brain".

To do this, sit somewhere you won't be disturbed. You can sit on the floor cross legged on the heels in Vajra Asana or sit upright in a chair. Make sure that your back is as straight as possible and that your head is erect and not drooping forward.

Clasp the hands together with the right hand dominant over the left. Alternatively place them on the thighs. Close the eyes and begin to focus the attention on the breath. Just be aware of the movement of the breath as you breathe in and out through the nose, paying attention to the passage of the breath, the movement of your body as you breathe in and out, and the sensation of the air entering and leaving your body.

After a few breaths of simple observation, try to slow the breath down. An ideal goal is to extend the inhalation and exhalation to a 6 second count each, but if you are new to this practice this might be hard at first. Simply try to slow the breath, and keep the in and out breath equal in length. If you can take the breath to a 6 second count then do so, but if not, keep that in mind as the goal of your practice eventually (over time and practice you will expand your lung capacity and will be able to take the breath to 6 seconds in length).

Keep this practice going for as long as you can. When your mind wanders, don't judge the thoughts, or yourself for having them, simply bring the focus of the mind back to the breath. We all have to do this; part of the skill that gets developed through this practice is less about the absence of the thoughts, but more about noticing them and coming back to focussing on the breath. I have been practicing this for a long time now, and still have to often bring my thoughts back to my breath - what has changed is that I become aware of my wandering mind sooner, and don't get dejected by it and give up thinking 'oh, I can't do this'.

Practising this regularly will help you to quieten the mind when you need peace, and will, in time, lead to a more peaceful, quieter mind in general.

There is a video which can guide you through this process in the bonus pack that accompanies this book, for more details and to get access to the material, please go to http://bit.ly/bent_shape.

*Sukha Purvaka Pranayama*

Full Sukha Purvaka Pranayama is performed in four stages, each building on the previous stage. About 4 rounds of each stage should be performed in each sitting, and the next stage only attempted when that is comfortable.

Sukha Purvaka Pranayama is the simplest form of Pranayama. It is the first type that needs to be mastered by the before other more advanced forms of Pranayama should be attempted. It is performed in a seated position, preferably Vajra Asana. If this is uncomfortable for the body, a hard backed chair which forces the body to be upright may be used. Alternatively, another seated posture could be used such as Baddha Konasana, the Tailor's Posture.

Full Sukha Purvaka Pranayama is performed in four stages, each building on the previous stage.

The first stage is the simple Sukha Pranayama. A healthy adult with no respiratory conditions should comfortably be able to perform all the stages of Sukha Purvaka Pranayama to a count of 6 or 8 (seconds) for both the in and out breath. A child or adult with respiratory difficulties should use a count of 4. At no time should either the in or out breath cause strain or stress. If this is the case, a lower count should be used until the lung capacity is increased. The length of the in and out breath should always be the same, whatever the length of the breath.

IN --------------- OUT ------------IN ------------OUT

The second stage of Sukha Purvaka Pranayama is called Visama Vritta, or Loma Pranayama. In this stage, the in breath is held for the same length of count as the in and out breath, forming a cycle of in-hold-out.

IN -------- HOLD -------- OUT ------------- IN ------- HOLD ------- OUT

In the third phase, or Viloma Pranayama, the in breath is released immediately at the end of the in count, and the out breath is held, reversing the process of the second stage. The pattern of the cycle for this stage is in-out-hold.

IN ------- OUT ------ HOLD -------- IN ------- OUT ------- HOLD -------

The fourth and final stage combines the breath and the holds to create a four-part breath cycle of in-hold-out-hold. As with all the other stages, the breaths and the hold must all be of the same length.

IN -------HOLD---- OUT ------ HOLD --------IN -----HOLD---- OUT ------
- HOLD -------

An adult with respiratory conditions restricting their Pranayama breath count should hope to find that, with time and regular, committed practice, they are able to increase their count and see an improvement in their condition as their breathing technique improves and their lung capacity increases.

## Pranayama and relaxation

There are many types of relaxation that Yoga offers to help us calm the mind and body and each of them involve a focus on the breath in some way. In this next section I am going to describe a few of the simplest relaxation practices that Yoga offers, they may be simple, but it does not mean that they are not effective; they are some of my favourite practices in my own relaxation, and standard favourites within my classes.

## Shava Asana

The practices below require that the body is put into a posture known as Shava Asana. It is the ultimate relaxation posture. To get into this posture, lie flat on the floor, preferably with the head pointing to the North. Place a blanket over the body, as the body temperature drops during relaxation and you won't be able to relax if you are cold.

Making sure the body is in a straight line, bring the arms alongside the body, as close to the body as possible, with the palms facing upwards. Bring the ankles together, and allow the feet to splay open so that the feet are relaxed. Gently bring the chin lightly towards the chest, keeping the head on the floor, so that the neck is straight. Close the eyes, and begin your chosen relaxation practice.

This can be the simple technique of focussing on the breath, detailed above in the 'quiet sitting' section, it can be a more involved practice (see below).

## Savitri Pranayama

The word 'Savitri' means both rhythm and harmony. Savitri Pranayama is a rhythmic breath that harmonises mind, body and soul. While there are many other forms of Rhythmic Breaths that can be learned, this is the most beneficial and important.

Savitri Pranayama consists of four parts. Purakha - the inhalation, Kumbhaka - the breath held in, Rechaka - the exhalation, and Shunyaka - the breath held out.

In the classical version of Savitri Pranayama, the breath cycle is performed to a ratio of 2x1. This means for every 2 counts of breath in or out, the breath is held in or out for a count of 1. There is a range of different counts, or Tala, that can be employed for Savitri Pranayama. The choice of count used would depend to a large extent on the age, size or general health of the individual. As the different Tala also give different benefits to health and wellbeing, a person might work towards perfecting a particular Tala to reap the specific benefits it offers, although this work would need to be done in a methodical, step by step manner.

For an asthmatic, someone recovering from surgery, suffering from heart problems or a child, the 2 Tala (4x2x4x2) is a very beneficial Tala as it promotes growth by stimulating the glands, and increases lung capacity and breath control. It should not be done indefinitely though, a person starting their pranayama journey with a 2 Tala should, with practice and time, be able to practice longer Talas for increased benefit.

The 3 Tala (6.3.6.3) is the best for getting the maximum amount of Prana into the body, and for balancing erratic mood swings, so would be very good for someone in addiction recovery. It is the one I sometimes teach in my classes. This would be the preferred Tala for a teenager, small woman or someone at the start of their Pranayama learning.

The 4 Tala (8x4x8x4) is very good for strengthening the body. It is also good for meditation and calming the body. Regular practice of this will bring about general optimum health in the body.

The 5 Tala (10x5x10x5) will benefit those with poor circulation and will increase the metabolism, making this beneficial for anyone struggling to lose weight. This Tala also helps to overcome laziness and procrastination, so is good for a person who finds these traits problematic.

The 6 Tala (12x6x12x6) is good for enhancing the senses, memory and clarity of mind.

The 7 Tala (14x7x14x7) is also called Santosha Pranayama, the Serenity Breath. It promotes calmness and serenity, and is an excellent Tala for meditation.

The 8 Tala (16x8x16x8) is a very advanced Pranayama known as Siddha Pranayama, the Master's Breath. This Tala promotes longevity and good health, and is also associated with high ideals.

For someone learning Pranayama, it is important to work through the Talas in order, perfecting the breath in each and practising them at length before moving on to the next. It is better to gain mastery of one than perform them all badly. Indeed, it can damage the lung if we try to practice a longer tala before we are ready – I once tried to practice a 5 Tala, thinking my lungs had improved sufficiently to do so, and I think I actually pulled a muscle! I was in significant discomfort with every breath for a couple of days while it healed. If you wish to practice Savitri Pranayama, and I do recommend it, please take it slowly and listen to your body!

Once you have gone through at least 9 rounds of Savitri Pranayama, relax in Shava Asana for at least 10 minutes to get the full benefits of this deep relaxation.

## Marmanasthanam Kriya

The Marmanasthanam Kriya is a relaxation technique that involves conscious concentration on the 22 sensitive parts of the body which are grouped together and called Marmanasthanam. This invokes a very deep sense of relaxation in the body and mind. It has two purposes, depending on the way in which it is performed. When started at the feet it is a relaxation exercise, when started at the head it promotes concentration.

The relaxation is performed in Shava Asana after 9 rounds of Savitri Pranayama have been performed. Beginning at the feet, the awareness is taken to different parts of the body in turn, commanding that body part to relax. This can simply involve thinking of the relevant body part, then thinking the word 'relax'

The order of the body parts is (1) toes (2) feet (3) calves to knee (4) thighs (5) buttocks (6) base of spine (7) pelvic area (8) abdomen (9) chest 10) shoulders (11) fingers (12) hands (13) lower arms and elbows (14) upper arms and shoulders (15) throat (16) mouth and chin (17) nose and cheeks (18) eyes (19) back of the ears (20) back of the head (21) top of the head (22) Cavernous Plexus in the middle of the forehead (between the eyebrows).

To perform this as a concentration technique, reverse the sequence starting from number 21 to 1, then returning the awareness to the cavernous plexus.

Following this focussed relaxation exercise, remain in Shava Asana for at least 10 minutes to allow the body to absorb the benefits of the deep relaxation.

If you can learn to relax the body and mind, you will find that the rest of life becomes so much easier, as you sleep better, have more energy, deal with stress better and function better in every way in the body and mind.

More information about pranayama, including some relaxation MP3 recordings, are available in the bonus pack that accompanies this book, further details can be found at http://bit.ly/bent_shape.

# Conclusion

I was surprisingly taken aback when Lisa, my editor, asked me how I was going to write my conclusion. I hadn't actually planned a conclusion. Ending things well has never been one of my strong points, in life as well as in my writing. I knew I needed to, but had no idea how.

I emailed her back; *"Conclusion – not a clue as yet – I was never any good at conclusions, always seeming to prefer to fizzle away, or just keep rambling on! ☺It will come to me ☺"*

I then had a post Yoga, pre Marcus waking up bath with this month's Yoga magazine, *Yoga Life,* as my chosen reading. I was delighted to read the editorial written by Ammaji. It was as if, through her, Swami Gitananda was telling me what the conclusion of this book had to be.

The words I read seemed so perfectly timed;

*"One must learn to gracefully let go of things, of people, of places, of situations. Don't hold on. Just lightly let things happen and lightly deal with them. Let go! Let flow! Let God! For anything new to begin, the old must end. All change implies the 'old' must be released to 'give space' for the 'new'".*

As I read this paragraph over and over, I realised that this was the lesson I needed to take for the difficult process of ending this book, just as surely as it was the process by which the story in this book, as well as the book itself, developed.

In order to break free of the addiction that had blighted my life for so many years. I had to let go of such a lot; tension, habits, attachments to substances, to people, to situations, to places. I had to learn to let go of thought patterns, to allow things to happen and to deal with them, instead of raging against the world and feeling powerless. I had to let go of a lot of fears that I wouldn't be able to sleep, deal with stress, to have fun, to have friendships or enjoy socialising without alcohol.

I had to let go of a lot of ideas I had about the place of alcohol in my life. I had to let go of the identity I had created for myself, an identity I didn't like, but that was the only one I knew. This letting go was scary at first, but, as Swamiji says, in the space this letting go gave me, I was able to create a new life, a new identity, new coping techniques, new friendships and new ways to have fun. While letting go was hard and scary at first, the effects of that letting go have been such a blessing – at no point have I felt that I have lost anything by giving up drinking and smoking, I only see how much I have gained.

A great deal of letting go went in to the act of writing this book. Procrastination, laziness, doubt, perfectionism, and above all, fear (so much fear - fear of criticism, fear that I am getting it all wrong, fear that the book isn't academic enough, fear that I am 'getting above myself' in thinking I can or should write this book, fear of revealing too much about myself, fear of not revealing enough, fear that my words weren't making sense... the list is endless).

I had to accept that this book isn't going to be the ground-breaking marriage of modern Western scientific understanding and ancient

Eastern wisdom that I had originally envisioned. I am not a psychologist, not a neuroscientist, I am not an addiction expert and have only been a yoga teacher for a short while. I am years from having the understanding necessary to enable me to *that* book. I had to accept that *this* is the book that I am writing, and that this book is good enough.

I had to let go of the idea that I was going to write the next 'Eat Pray Love', and all the other absurd fantasies that my ego created in my mind, which, far from inspiring me, created ridiculous panic in me.

I somehow managed to let go of all this just enough to get to this point where I am now looking at the manuscript of my first (but not last!) book, and the sense of satisfaction is enormous, far stronger than any of the fears that nearly meant the book didn't get written.

During the writing process I also let go of a lot of emotions about, and attachment to, what I was writing. I have had revelations about myself and my life that I have wanted to share, but then realised that in sharing many elements of my story, I would also be sharing too much of other people's stories. I have had to work out a balancing act between Satya, truthfulness, and Ahimsa, non-harming. Sharing these truths may have hurt others, or may have hurt myself, so I have let go of many, many words, some of which I really struggled to remove as they made me cry, or made me proud, and my ego wanted to keep them in so you would think 'look how beautifully she writes, it made me cry'. I let that go. In a book that is, to a very large extent, about my experiences it is hard to keep the ego in check. I hope I have done that enough that it hasn't felt that it is 'all about me'.

Trying to end this is a real lesson in letting go. I keep thinking of things I haven't said, points I haven't made, concepts that haven't made it into the book. The beauty of Yoga is that it really is *the gift that keeps giving*, that every time you return to the teachings, it will offer you something different. I think I could write this book on a yearly basis and it would never be the same book twice. My understanding of the Yoga concepts, my experience of the practice and my understanding of the science will deepen every time. I have had to accept that if I try to share every thought and insight I get, then the only person who will ever experience this book will be me, and that is not the point of it at all.

All I can do in writing this book is 'do my best, and leave the rest'. I have written the best book I can write at the moment, and while I hope it helps you, I cannot guarantee it. I have to let it go and allow it to do what it will. I would like to end by sharing some of my hopes, what I would love, in the perfect world, for this book to have done for you.

If you are currently battling addiction issues, or are wondering if you have a problem that needs addressing, I hope that I have helped you to see that speaking about the problem can help. The stigma that surrounds addiction is so dangerous, dangerous to the person with the addiction, to those around them, and to society as a whole. If a society is judged on how it treats its most vulnerable, then the way we treat addicts speaks volumes about us. As I have already shared, addiction comes not through choice but out of pain. People should never be punished for being pain, or for asking for help in dealing with that pain. I think that we can change the attitudes of society by speaking out, by showing the world that just because you are an addict, or used to be addicted, that doesn't mark you as a bad person. We can rise above the stereotypes. I am not saying here that you have to, if you don't feel comfortable or safe to speak out then of course you shouldn't, but do try to find someone you trust that you can talk to.

If you are looking for a way to deal with some of the stresses and strains that addiction causes, whether as an addict yourself or as someone close to an addict, I hope that you can see that Yoga has many tools that can help you to relax your body and mind. There are many more relaxation and breathing techniques than I have described here, find a good yoga teacher who places priority on teaching about the breath and relaxing the body. Remember that whatever happens in life, 'all this will pass', and never forget the value of taking a breath before reacting to any situation. Sometimes that space between event and reaction can be all we need to completely change our perception of a problem.

I hope that I have shown that a life of addiction doesn't mean that you have nothing to contribute or that you are in some way a weak person. What we get through in life teaches us many lessons, if we are open to learning them. The recovered addicts I have met are some of the strongest people I know. When you emerge from the shame, self-loathing and violence of addiction, you emerge stronger than you were before. Another article in the Yoga Life magazine quotes Napoleon Hill, in a quote that could be destined for this book!

*"The strongest oak of the forest is not the one that is protected from the storm and hidden from the sun, it is the one who stands in the open where it is compelled to struggle for its existence against the winds and rains and the scorching heat."*

As an addict you may feel that you are weak, I remember that feeling well, but you are not, you have strength in you that you just cannot access. Yoga might not be the solution for you, but I know that somewhere there is a solution that will work for you. There is a solution for everyone. Yoga might offer you some tools to add to your toolbox along the way and I hope that you will find something of value in the practices, ideas and thoughts I have shared.

I end with the Shanti Mantra that is chanted at the end of every Yoga class I have taught and attended since discovering Gitananda Yoga. I love chanting this, the sounds are beautiful, and its meaning is wonderful. Marcus and I sing it every night at bedtime. This is my message to you.

**Aum**
**Lokah Samastha Sukhinu Bhavantu**
**Sarvaa Janaha Sukhinu Bhavantu**
**Aum Shanthi Shanthi Shanthi**
**Aum**
**Aum**

May all beings be happy and at ease.

May all beings be wise and may they evolve gracefully into higher realms of consciousness.

May all beings possess peace in their bodies, in their minds and in their consciousness.

May all beings experience the peace which surpasses understanding, the peace of the Divine Light

**Aum, Peace, Peace, Peace, Aum**

## Stay in touch

As I have said earlier in the book, helping others beat addiction through Yoga is my life's purpose. If you want or need help, then I want to help you.

I have begun to create a library of resources that you can access as a thank you for purchasing this book, simply visit http://bit.ly/bent_shape and register to get access.

# Appendix

## Gitananda Yoga teachers across the world

If reading this book has inspired you to want to try Gitananda Yoga, you are in luck! Hundreds of students have passed through the 6-month training in Ananda Ashram and are teaching all over the world. You can find teachers across the world listed at icyer.com/Teachers.php. You will not regret bringing Gitananda Yoga into your life, and may find, like I did, that it opens up a whole new world to you! Please let me know if you do, I would love to hear about your experience!

## A selection of posts from my blog

I write sporadically on my website blog about things that cross my mind and that I feel the need to share. I am not as disciplined with this as I ought to be, a combination of the procrastination, perfectionism, and an inner critic that seem to be my constant companions when I write, conspire to mean that there are many half-finished, or finished but not published. I have posts littering the drafts section of the site and my documents folder on my laptop! They nearly stopped this book being written, but for the time being at least, I seem to have managed to work out how to conquer them.

Here are a few of the posts that are most relevant to this book. I have, in general, left them as they are, removing only the calls to action that came at the end of the posts (they have not been edited for this book, I wanted to keep them authentically how I wrote them at the time, as they are part of my journey).

There is a great deal of interest in 'mindfulness' these days. It is not surprising, we have so much stimulation around us constantly, so much pressure, so much to do, our poor brains are completely overworked trying to process it all. We need to become more mindful, to slow ourselves and our minds down, to reduce the stimulation we put our mind through.

I have been told a couple of times that I should 'do Mindfulness', that it would be good for me, good for my business.

My response is that I already am.

'Mindfulness' is all about teaching people how to be in the present moment, how to live now instead of worrying about the past or future. This is the only way to truly live happily, as dwelling on the past, or worrying about, or constantly living in the future, generally leads us to unhappiness. If we are so busy planning and dreaming about our future, we can miss the joys and opportunities life has to offer us right now.

I was really bad at this until recently. I was fairly convinced I was suffering from Bipolar Disorder, as my mind was constantly racing, with sometimes so many thoughts racing around my head I felt that I was going to explode. There would be the opposite sensation, feeling so utterly empty I wondered if I was even still in my mind. This was never a peaceful silence, but a very frightening sense of being utterly lost and of total misery. I was so fearful for the future, particularly for my children, so scared of climate change, growing global inequality, worried that I had no idea how to prepare Marcus for a future I couldn't even begin to imagine, that I was miserable, bad tempered, incredibly negative, and always distracted.

I failed to spot that the best hope I could give to Marcus was to focus on him right now, make sure that he feels loved, secure, and give him a happy childhood. Now, I have changed my viewpoint, and while all the things I mentioned still scare me, I don't focus on them. I spend far better time with Marcus, and we are learning to grow vegetables together, exploring nature together, and he is far happier and confident than he was. All of which will stand him in much better stead for the future, whatever it might throw at him.

I owe this new way of looking at the world very much to my Yoga practice.

Yoga is the very best tool for practicing and teaching 'mindfulness'. Every single aspect of it requires at least an attempt at mindfulness, it teaches us how to control and still the mind with every step we take along the Yoga path.

We work a lot with the breath in Yoga. This simple practice of observing and slowing the breath, keeping our focus on the breath, forcing the breath to behave in a certain way, as many of the practices require, brings us very firmly into the present. We learn to control the power our thoughts have over us by practicing returning the attention to the breath when we get distracted. Slowing the breath slows the mind, bringing us to a place of peace and stillness in both body and mind.

One of the added bonuses of mindfulness through yoga is that you get the multitude of physical benefits to the body as well as the stilling of the mind. Our Asana practice is not simply about toning the muscles of the body, it brings us very much into our body, into the moment, into a mindful state. It is virtually impossible to balance well when the mind is distracted by thoughts, so to be able to balance we must be in a calm, peaceful mental state. Some of the Asanas we practice such as Veera Asana (known in the West as The Warrior Pose) are good for developing concentration and focus. All the Asanas work with the breath and so continue to develop the focus referred to above.

Yoga places a great deal of importance on 'self study'. Through a regular Yoga practice, you will probably come to find that you quite naturally start to make healthier choices about what you do with and to your body, that you start to listen to your body's cues better. You will find that as you become calmer that your mind becomes calmer and less noisy, more 'mindful'.

Yoga places a massive amount of importance on relaxation of body and mind. Throughout a class I will ask my students to relax their body and focus on the breath after doing postures. This is a very important part of the process of Gitananda Yoga as it teaches the body and mind the difference between tension and relaxation. With the focus again returning to the breath, and the tension that is being released from the body, our 'mindfulness muscles' are getting a workout as we are very much focussed on the 'now'.

Many people associate meditation with Yoga. While meditation is a part of Yoga, in the Gitananda system of Yoga we do not talk about 'doing meditation'. Meditation is one of the highest practices of Yoga, it is second only to Samadhi, enlightenment, in the Eight Limbs of Yoga. This can only be achieved through achieving competence in the six other stages of Yoga, through clean, ethical living (Yamas and Niyamas), a healthy body (Asana), exquisite control over the breath (Pranayama), control of the senses (Pratyahara), and the ability to concentrate deeply to the exclusion of all external and internal distractions (Dharana). Only then can we achieve Dhyana, meditation. While western Meditation is highly beneficial as it helps to slow the mind, I will not talk about anything I teach in class as being meditation.

If you want to become more mindful, if your mind is feeling overwhelmed by the noise, busy-ness and constant stimulation of the outside world, and our inner 'chitter chatter' of the ever working mind, simply close your eyes (when safe and appropriate to do so, obviously!), and focus on your breath, Try to keep the in and out breath even, try to fill the lungs completely, and empty them completely, and keep your attention focussed on the breath. It really helps to count the breaths in your mind, as this helps to keep the attention on the breath. If you can get to a slow 6 count (one second per number) then that is great, if not, work with what you can – as you practice this you will find that your lung capacity will increase.

The beauty of this practice is that it can be done very informally, so can be done at your desk in work. and with adaption can be done anywhere. When stuck in traffic, we can slow the breath, with the eyes open, it isn't quite the same, but it will certainly help to calm down your frazzled nerves.

Mindful or mind full? I know what I prefer, and I am very grateful to my Yoga practice for helping me achieve greater peace and space in my far too busy mind.

### 3 July 2015, Was I really an alcoholic?

I have only really talked about my drinking problem since it has been something in my past. I started to talk freely to people about how much I worried about my drinking once I had made the decision that I was stopping, the last time I decided that!

I have been quite surprised at how little people closest to me knew about how much I drank. Yes, my friends knew I drank to excess in their company, usually flaking out and passing into an unwakeable sleep. Yes, my parents knew that I was often very groggy if they called me 'early' in the morning at weekends. Yes, my family knew that I would always very enthusiastically greet the alcohol at any family event. Yes, anyone who visited my house would often see recycling bags full of cider cans and wine bottles.

They all knew this, but it seems that no one apart from Liam, my son, put all the pieces together to work out that I actually had a major problem. And who can blame them? I was the only person who really knew the full extent of my drinking, and I think I even managed to keep myself fairly in the dark about it.

Well, that last bit isn't entirely true, I knew perfectly well that I was powerless in the face of my cravings, that I could think to myself 'I'm not going to drink tonight', but that wouldn't necessarily mean that I wouldn't end up with a can of cider or glass on wine in my hand later. I was very conscious that not drinking on a particular evening always meant a conscious decision rather than 'normal' behaviour.

I chose to think I could always deal with it another time, and that tonight, I really 'deserved' my drink. I think that fact alone makes the answer to the question in the title of this post fairly obvious!

Since my yoga based recovery from alcoholism, I have begun to feel comfortable about talking about my alcoholism. This is something that was not the case before. It is something I have started freely talking to friends and family about, always in the past tense, as I no longer feel like the same person that I was. I have not 'given up alcohol', through Yoga I have seen another way to approach life that doesn't need alcohol, and I no longer need to hide myself in a bottle of wine. The alcoholic Esther is a thing of the past.

Recently, when we were out walking together, my mother asked me how, as I was able to give up drinking completely during the time I was pregnant and breastfeeding my youngest son, could I consider that I had been an alcoholic. Surely I wasn't as bad as I was imagining I was.

This was an interesting question, and one I struggled to answer in a way that I found satisfying. I needed to ponder it some more.

I gave up drinking easily when pregnant, I couldn't have been an alcoholic, could I?

I knew why I was able to eliminate alcohol completely once I knew I was having another child, aged 37. When I found out that I was pregnant, my initial reaction was not a good one. I was 36, would be 37 by the time the child was born, had only been with the father for a few months, and was already having some doubts about the relationship. I was at the time, a very heavy drinker and smoker, and knew that there was a good chance I had caused serious damage to my eggs over the years. My son's father was also a heavy drinker and had been for many years. I didn't know much about fetal alcohol syndrome, but knew that there was a chance that this child could suffer as result of alcohol. I decided that as I had made the decision to continue with the pregnancy, then I had to give my child the very best chance I possibly could. I stopped drinking and smoking immediately, and focussed all of my attention on nurturing this child, exercising, sleeping, eating well, to give my child the very best chance I could possibly give him.

When Marcus was born, there was never any question that he would be breastfed for as long as possible, as I knew that this was the best thing for him to ensure his health and good development. Throughout this time, I didn't drink or smoke, nor did I want to most of the time.

One night, Marcus's father and I arranged for Marcus to spend the night at my parents' house so that we could go out. I expressed a full day's worth of milk so that I would be able to have a 'well deserved' drink. We didn't go far, we went to the nearest pub.

After over a year of sobriety, I must have drunk at least a bottle of red wine (impossible to say as it came from a box at the bar, but there were several large glasses). I didn't smoke however, my return to smoking came later.

As I lay in bed the next day, nursing a savage headache and feeling dreadful, I remember thinking that I had been really glad to have that drink, that I had missed it and that I was glad that I was now able to drink again.

It was like being reunited with the love of my life after a reluctant separation. Yes, I had made the choice to stop for the benefit of my child, because his life and wellbeing was, for the time that he depended directly on my body for his sustenance, bigger and more important than my need for drink. But the need never went away; it was just muted for a while. I was always going to revert to drinking, none of the problems I was trying to mask had gone away (and many new ones had presented themselves). I had paused my drinking, not given it up, I had never even thought about giving it up.

In pondering the question my mother asked me, I found a few tests online in response to the search question 'Am I an alcoholic?'. According to the tests I did, answering the way I would have if I had

• • •
156

been capable of such self-analysis and honesty back then, not only was I an alcoholic, but I was in serious need of urgent medical help!

I didn't seek medical help, I found my salvation through Yoga. It is because of what I learned through Yoga teacher training that I talk about my alcoholism in the past. I WAS an alcoholic, now I am a very different person. I think of 'old Esther' as a different person entirely, someone I had to be in order to be the Esther I am now. I look back at her with a range of emotions; anger, regret, disgust, shame, compassion, pity, love, hate.... I wish there were things she hadn't done and said, situations she hadn't got herself into, damage to herself and others that hadn't been caused, but I don't really regret any of it, as it was all vital to get me to where I am now.

*16 July 2015, Resilience to stress through Yoga*

I wrote my dissertation for my Yoga teacher training course about how Yoga can help people deal better with, and learn to control, stress in their lives. This was a crucial discovery for me through my training, and I have had several examples through the last year when I KNOW I have dealt with situations far better than I would have previously.

However, in the last week, I have been in a situation that has really clearly shown me how much better I deal with stressful situations in my own life, and how Yoga has altered every aspect of my response to stress.

From the very start of this situation, I have been conscious that I have been reacting very differently than 'pre Gitananda Yoga' Esther would have. Back then I would have got angry, got emotional, cried, shouted, sent ill-advised text messages, got into a pointless and counterproductive text/email/Facebook argument, smoked copious amounts of cigarettes, drank wine, ranted and raged (in person and probably on Facebook) and been very tense and distracted in the presence of the people I was with at the weekend.

Instead, I was calm and collected throughout. I didn't do any of the things mentioned above at all. I was calm, peaceful, content and present with the people who needed me all through the weekend. I slept well, I laughed, I played, I read ALL of Charlie and the Chocolate Factory (not to myself, to Marcus, who was an utterly enraptured audience!) and most of all, I was relaxed and happy the whole time.

There are two changes in my life that I can thank for this changed response to a stressful situation.

The first is the fact that I no longer drink and smoke. I used to use these two poisons to 'help' me to get through difficult situations. I thought they helped me, but they really didn't, they made everything so much harder. The cigarettes were, among many other problems, drastically reducing the amount of vital oxygen my body was receiving, preventing all parts of my body, including my brain, from functioning the way they should. Cigarettes told me that when I was stressed I needed them, and that if I inhaled the mix of chemicals they contained deeply into my lungs, then I would be calmed.

Until the craving for the next one that is, then I would be anxious because of my situation AND because I wanted a cigarette.

Alcohol told me that any stressful situation could be made less stressful with wine. It was very convincing, the first glass would always take the edge off the stress, the second more so, the 3rd and 4th slowly reducing my ability to process the stress, and the 5th, 6th etc. rendering me incapable of caring, or articulating. The hangover the next day would have seriously compromised my ability to be fully present and engaged with Marcus the following morning.

Neither of these ever really helped me deal with a problem in my life, they helped me bury my head in the sand and generally made the problems worse.

The second change is my integration of Yoga into my daily life; it is not simply something I do for a living; it has become a major part of my way of living. Yoga has given me many tools that help me during times of great stress, particularly the ability to breathe deeply and provide my body with the oxygen it needs to be able to function well, but I am grateful on a daily basis, an hourly basis even, that it helped me find the way to freedom from my demons.

*22 July 2015, 10 reasons I am happy to be sober*

I stopped drinking 9 months and 10 days ago, after about 20 years of dangerous, dependent drinking. I thought I needed alcohol, and her best friend nicotine, to help me deal with my life, but I started to see that these 'friends' were actually causing huge problems in my life, and making everything so much worse.

I have never regretted my decision of October 12 to stop drinking completely. At the time I made it, I did have small doubts that I would want it to be a complete cutting of the ties between me and alcohol, but I soon realised that there were far more compelling reasons to stay sober than there were to drink.

This was made possible thanks to The Om Studio's Yoga Teacher Training. Through the extensive work I did clearing long held stress and tension, learning to control my stress response, reprogramming my mind to think differently and making peace with a great deal from my past, going back into my earliest memories. There was much I needed to clear there, many seemingly innocuous or fairly insignificant incidents that had left deep scars in my psyche, and left me feeling like I needed to hide from the world and myself. Yoga helped me to see that I didn't need to let those scars continue to hurt me, that I could acknowledge them and be grateful for them, for they make me who I am today, and I am now very happy with that person!

There are so many reasons I am happy to be sober, and to joyfully tell people "I don't drink anymore". Here are some of them...

## 1. I get far more done

When I was drinking, I would, most nights, put Marcus (and previously Liam) to bed, then go downstairs and crack open the can or bottle that was to be my company for the night. Often I would do other things while drinking, but I was never as effective or productive as when I work sober. I completed a teaching degree like this, and got a 2:1 – I have often wondered what I would have been capable of had I not relied so heavily on cider to 'help' me with my assignments!

## 2. I am much less stressed and angry

This is such a big one! I used my stress and rage against the world, and specific people in it, to 'justify' my drinking. It is only now that I no longer do that, I can see that while I thought I was soothing my stress through drinking, I was actually making it so much worse. The liver is associated with anger in Yoga, and many other ancient medicine systems, and high stress and bad temper is associated with alcoholism.

I was often creating the stress I was trying to hide from. If I was up late drinking on a 'school night' because I'd 'had a stressful day', I would normally wake late, groggy, and unable to function properly the following morning, leading to a stressful start to the day for me and the boys. This would lead me to be bad tempered with the children in the morning as I tried to hurry them so I could make up time, and in the evening when I'd come home tired and grouchy after a foggy, stressful day at work, and the whole cycle would start again.

Now, I get up before the boys in the morning, and our mornings are peaceful and calm, as are our evenings.

## 3. I sleep

I LOVE my bed. I love bedtime.

This wasn't always the case. I have had problems sleeping since childhood, when irrational fears that we were all going to be murdered in our beds kept me awake every night after watching a film that frightened me. This was a problem from about the age of 8 perhaps, until I moved into a flat of my own with Josh. Then I found that my inner voice shifted focus, and instead of telling me a stranger was going to break in and murder me for no reason, it started to tell me all the reasons I was a terrible person, to remind me of all the stupid things I had ever done, or to fill my head with grand dreams and excitements, and to make sure sleep was never going to be easy. Yoga could have helped me with this, had I known, but instead I apparently decided it was far easier to stay up really late and have a 'few cans' to help me sleep. But of course, alcoholic sleep is not sleep, you pass out and then it is very hard to wake afterwards, because you have not had a proper, refreshing sleep.

Now, I go to bed very early, sometimes at the same time as putting Marcus to bed, sometimes later, depending on how I feel and what I have to do. I read for a while, then sleep. I sleep well. I often remember my dreams. And I can wake up in a split second if Marcus needs me. I wake feeling refreshed and happy, and never feel stressed on waking

## 4. I like myself

This is completely new for me! I have never really been happy with who I am, always had such a strong feeling of not fitting in, not being totally accepted by the majority of people, and always felt very unhappy about this, seeing this as meaning that there was something wrong and profoundly unlikable about me.

I now know that this is ok, I like my 'weirdness', and know that as long as the people who are really important in my life get me and love me, then it doesn't matter what society as a whole thinks of me.

I have been able to make peace with my past; with the many things I have done that I regret. I no longer regret much that I have done or that has happened in my life, I have taken lessons from it all, and every single one of those 'regrets' have helped to form who I am today.

## 5. I enjoy my own company

I used to HATE being by myself. I used to feel very lonely and unhappy when alone, as though being alone was proof that no one liked me.

When I was alone the inner critic that seemed to really despise me would get really loud, and give me no peace. I drank to try to drown her out, but it usually made her louder. Now, I rarely hear from her, and when I do, I know how to ignore her, or listen to what she says and decide if I need to pay heed to what she is saying (sometimes she does make good points!).

Now I find I am able to be alone quite happily, and I actually enjoy it. I no longer feel lonely just because I am alone. I am in the company of someone who finally has my best interests at heart!

## 6. My liver and digestive system love me

My poor liver has taken such a beating over the years, between the alcohol at night and the coffee and junk food I used to get me through each day. I spent many a day being acutely aware of a throbbing ache in my liver that clearly indicated I had hugely overdone it.

The liver has such a key role in our health, we need it to be healthy for everything else in our body to function well. Fortunately, it is the one organ that can regenerate and heal itself. I don't know how long it takes to heal, I think it depends on how damaged it is to start, but I am reasonably confident that after 9 months' booze free, with healthy eating and plenty of hydration, my liver is now in a significantly better state than it was.

My abdomen was swollen far beyond the tummy I have had since puberty, this can only have been my liver and digestion struggling to cope with the demands put upon them. since stopping drinking, I no longer suffer with this discomfort, or the almost permanently upset tummy I used to have when I drank a lot of cider (Strongbow is no friend to the digestive system!). I still have a bit of a belly, but it is nowhere near as prominent as it was, and I have come to accept that as the 42-year-old mother of 3, it is FINE for me to have a belly, I even quite like it sometimes!

## 7. I look better

Drinking and smoking take their toll on your appearance, the toxins in the substances, combined with the late nights I was having. I look at photos from my drinking days and I now think I look dreadful, even in the photos I liked at the time! People who have not seen me for some time often comment on how good I look. I think the combination of the elimination of negative habits, the increase of positive habits (I practice Yoga nearly every day, I walk often, I eat better, I drink lots of herbal tea and water, I don't eat so much junk food), and the fact that I am HAPPY all contribute to make me look so much better than I ever did before! I like the way I look now, that is a new and enjoyable change in my life, I used to hate looking at myself before!

## 8. I feel healthier physically and mentally

This is not just down to stopping drinking, but to my integration of Yoga into my life. Yoga was definitely pivotal in helping me be able to stop drinking, and smoking, and it has led me to try to live a healthier life in general. But giving up drinking has led to me being healthier in both body and mind.

My body is certainly in far better condition than it was before. Giving up smoking, combined with learning to breathe correctly, has made a massive difference to the asthma I have had since childhood. I have more energy to do the things I want and need to do, even though I generally go to bed really early by my previous standards. But it is my mental health that has benefitted most from giving up drinking I think.

I was getting to be very concerned about my mental health before I started my Yoga teacher training. Having almost certainly come through a nervous breakdown in 2013 (possibly still in its grip), I felt like I was completely falling apart, something I had almost been waiting for since completing my degree in 2001. Having completed a respected test I had been given by a friend, I seemed to score highly for Bipolar Disorder, something I had suspected for a very long time, with racing thoughts and manic elated highs, and very frightening lows where I felt empty and 'missing' somehow.

Now, I no longer get the extremes of emotion, find my thoughts far easier to follow and ignore when I need to, and have not had a very low day for many, many months, I don't remember the last one. I am sure that my mental health problems were being massively exacerbated by my drinking, and now that I don't do that, and have learned many yoga practices that help me keep myself grounded, I feel OK mentally almost all of the time.

## 9. I no longer smoke

As an asthmatic who had harangued her father into giving up smoking as a child, I knew I should never have taken up smoking. But with my finger on the self-destruct button from a fairly early age, I suppose it was inevitable I was going to (as a child I was also never going to drink, and was fervently anti-drugs – both of those faded to nothing as I got older)

While I used to smoke during the days, I often whittled my smoking down to 'only' when I was having a drink. Of course, these two habits then fed each other completely – if I wanted to drink I would smoke, and I would use a craving for a cigarette as an excuse to buy wine, so I could smoke! I tended to smoke a lot more when drinking too, as if I was making up for the cigarettes I hadn't smoked when not drinking!

I gave up smoking sporadically many times, sometimes lasting long periods of time. After starting my teacher training, I learned that smoking when learning to breathe better was more damaging as I was opening up my lungs and taking the smoke to places that had never experienced it before. I often managed to drink without smoking, but it was always an effort. I eventually realised that if I wanted to give up smoking for good, I was going to have to ditch the drinking. This made the decision to quit drinking that little bit harder as I was loath to say goodbye to my two 'crutches', but eventually it was the easiest decision to take – I wanted a good and healthy life, the two poisons in my life were stopping me achieve that.

## 10. My children have a better life

Marcus can't remember seeing me drink or drunk. Liam can, but he is an adult now, and has lots of memories of it. I am thrilled that Marcus will never see his mother in a state like I used to get into, will never know the frustration and pain of being left to his own devices while I recover on the sofa, doesn't have to endure me in a state every morning rushing him out of the house, late for school again.

By giving up drinking I have hopefully given my boys extra years of having their Mum around and capable of being there for them, reduced the chance of them having to watch me die a slow and painful death I have caused myself, and am a far better role model for them than I was previously.

I thought for many years that drinking was helping me get through my life, but I feel that my life has now really started to begin, with my finally in the driving seat, making my own decisions without my brain getting fogged with booze. I won't always make the right decisions, and that is fine, I will learn from my bad decisions, as I have learned from my decades of slow suicide. I am going to be exploring my journey to sobriety in far more detail in the coming weeks, and would love to hear from you if you have similar experiences to share, or similar worries about your own, or someone else's habits. Please post in the comments, or contact me privately if you would like to chat

*1 October 2015, Go Sober for Health and Happiness*

Trying to Go Sober in 2013

Two years ago I signed up to take part in Macmillan Cancer Support's Go Sober campaign. I had done quite a bit of fundraising for them in the past, and opted to do this not as a pubic fundraising venture, but as a private challenge. I needed to see if I could give up drinking. This was going to be a real challenge as I was not in a good mental state at the time, still reeling from the breakdown I had suffered from earlier in the year (probably still in its grip, and not asking anyone for help other than emotional support from friends and family – I was too scared to approach my doctor)

Day 1 was fine. Day 2 was ok. Day 3 was a challenge. I had to attend a family court hearing to resolve a really acrimonious separation and contact issues between my ex and I. It had been a horrible experience that I found incredibly difficult, stressful and distressing.

After the hearing, I went to my best friend's house to rant and rage. She immediately offered me a glass of wine, our standard shared response to this sort of stress. I resisted for a minute, but then gave in, and drained the glass with relief. I had another glass, and walked home, buying a bottle on the way. I told myself that I would start #gosober again the next day, but the reality was I was already starting to suspect that I would not be able. After a few more days I stopped even trying, and drank as much that month as I would have otherwise.

My experiment to see if I could quit had proved quite conclusively that I couldn't. I was starting to have to accept, after about 20 years of alcohol dependence, that I did indeed have the problem I had been trying to ignore.

### Sober in October

Last October, I didn't sign up for Go Sober, but, through my Yoga Teacher Training, I was already reducing my alcohol intake, as I was feeling less and less that I needed alcohol to be able to relax, and I knew that I preferred waking up on mornings when I had gone to bed sober.

On October 12, after a really fun night of lots of wine, chat, music, dancing and silliness with my really good friend, I woke up with a savage hangover, utterly exhausted after not enough sleep, and realised I never wanted to experience this feeling ever again.

I was reluctant to tell myself that I was never going to drink ever again, as my natural self sabotaging tendencies would have immediately cried out for wine had I done that, but I made decisions every day that I wasn't going to drink. I also gave up smoking on that day, beginning a much needed healing of my asthma affected lungs.

When I was able to attend my brother's beautiful wedding, and opt for Elderflower sparkle instead of the expensive red wine that was freely available, and thoroughly enjoyed the night, I knew I had made a decision I could stick to, I could enjoy life sober.

Since then I have not even come close to relapse, I have never doubted for a second that I have made the right decision.

I am healthy and happy, the depression and self-loathing that fuelled my drinking for years seem to have abated, I have respect for myself and can stand my own company, and can bear to look at myself in the mirror. This is just too wonderful to want to risk losing.

I met up with a friend who I hadn't seen since I got sober, and she looked at me and said "You're a great advert for giving up drinking aren't you?" That made me really happy, because before I didn't look great at all!

I know that my recovery was all thanks to my Yoga practice. It was not just the physical work; I had done that for years without it making the slightest impact on my drinking habits. The realisation that Yoga is not just a form of exercise, but a system for living a good, healthy and happy life was a total game changer for me.

Yoga has helped me create the life I want, the life I am meant to live, the life I truly deserve. It has helped me to heal hurts that I have carried with me since childhood, to resolve the poor self-esteem that drove pretty much all of my self destructive behaviour. There is still work to be done, but I know what to do, and I know how to breathe through times when I feel emotions getting the better of me. I am daily grateful for my discovery of Gitananda Yoga, and for the great teaching I received from Kalavathi Devi at the Om Studio in Cardiff.

I love my life now I am sober, I have not looked back. Sober living isn't boring, indeed, I can now remember what I did last night, a real bonus!

*26th November 2015, Do you have the courage to find your truth?*

I just finished watching Eat Pray Love while cooking lunch. For some reason it has taken me a really long time to be able to watch this to the end – there has always been a reason why I stopped. I am currently reading the book as well, and have just listened to the audio book of 'Big Magic', so I have been a bit immersed in Liz Gilbert over the last couple of weeks.

This time of watching has really worked for me. Julia Roberts's portrayal of Liz's journey to self-discovery from real heartache and feeling lost has really touched me deeply. The words she speaks at the end of the film really made me cry and be glad I found Yoga, as they could have come from a Yoga book.

*In the end, I've come to believe in something I call "The Physics of the Quest". A force in nature governed by laws as real as the laws of gravity. The rule of Quest Physics goes something like this: If you're brave enough to leave behind everything familiar and comforting, which can be anything from your house to bitter, old resentments, and set out on a truth-seeking journey, either externally or internally, and if you are truly willing to regard everything that happens to you on that journey as a clue and if you accept everyone you meet along the way as a teacher and if you are prepared, most of all, to face and forgive some very difficult realities about yourself, then the truth will not be withheld from you.*

We hold on to so much that we think we need but that is actually holding us back from growth, from discovery of who we truly are, and from seeing the many possibilities that life has to offer us. I believe that "comfort zones" are what we create when we are scared of the unknown, scared of being hurt, scared to try new things. We don't have to live in fear, we are brave, strong souls who are here to find our true selves, not hide in our comfort zones.

When we were babies we weren't scared to try new things in the name of personal growth – we tried to walk and we fell over, we might have cried and needed a cuddle, but that didn't stop us, we kept trying and falling until we could just do it. At what point in life do we learn to be scared to try new things? Do we need to be scared?

Eleanor Roosevelt is quoted as saying "Do one thing every day that scares you", and I think this is truly great advice. When I stopped drinking it was scary, it meant a massive lifestyle change, and changes to pretty much all my relationships. It meant I had to find new ways to have fun, to deal with stress, to be in social situations, to make new friends. Most scary of all, I had to learn to be with myself completely, to stop hiding me from myself.

All those things were terrifying in the extreme, but I am so glad on a daily basis that I did them. My life is a million times better than it was, and it is going to keep getting better until it is over. I am constantly identifying things in my life I can and must let go of in order to grow and move further into the life I was born to live. Some are harder and scarier than others, but in time I will do it. I know it will be hard, and it will sometimes hurt, but in the space I will create in my life, great joy and happiness will come into it.

What are you holding onto in life out of fear that you could let go of?

*13th January 2016, Know yourself, Heal yourself – the great power of Self Study*

Aristotle has been credited with saying 'Knowing yourself is the beginning of all wisdom'. I don't know if he actually said this or not, but it is a popular internet meme, so it must be true eh?

Whether this famous philosopher said this or not, there is much truth and wisdom in the words. If we are looking to improve ourselves in any way at all, how can we even know where to begin if we don't know who we truly are?

When I was deeply immersed in my Yoga teacher training, one of the most time consuming, difficult but ultimately most rewarding part of the course was the 'Swadhyaya', the self-study that was an integral part of my development, personal growth and recovery from addiction.

What is Swadhyaya?

The journey of Self-study, or Swadhyaya, is one of the 5 Niyamas, the ethical observances that, when practiced well, teach us to become the best versions of ourselves that we can be. The Yamas take us beyond our animal instincts, and the Yamas elevate us to be better humans. In Patanjali's Yoga Sutras, Swadhyaya is identified as a way to connect us to the Divine, to discover the Divinity that exists in us all, which is the deepest goal of a life of Yoga.

**Study thy self, discover the divine.**

— Patanjali's Yoga Sutra, II.44

Swadhyaya is the process of looking deep into ourselves, and really seeing who we truly are. It is about becoming aware of our thoughts, actions, movement, habits, and motivations. It is awareness and understanding of our body and mind.

Patanjali tells us that through the practice of Kriya Yoga, a life devoted to Tapas (discipline), Swadhyaya (self Study) and Atman Pranidhana (surrendering to the Divine), Samadhi, or Enlightenment can be achieved, a 'fast track' to enlightenment if you will!

How can Swadhyaya help me?

Swadhyaya is the deep, and sometimes emotionally challenging and life changing, process of digging deep into ourselves and finding out who we truly are. It can help us to uncover patterns of behaviour that we have fallen into that might not be serving us well, it can help us identify where these patterns came from, and it can help us to work through the issues that might need to be cleared before we can release them. It can help us develop awareness of our body, our thoughts and our actions.

During the training, we were supposed to keep a journal of our experiences through the course. I didn't do this very well, as I have a huge aversion to keeping a diary, after former lovers have read things

I have written about my relationship with them and used them against me. I did, however, throw myself into the essay writing and used the directed nature of the essay questions to take my learning about Yoga into my understanding of myself, and would often write two or three times more than was expected in each essay as I allowed my subconscious to write for me. It was actually through this practice that I was able to identify the source of my problem with keeping a diary!

Swadhyaya helped me hugely through my journey to recovery, as it helped me work through the low self-esteem and emotional pain that led me to, and kept me in, addiction to alcohol. It gave me a safe space to process emotions that I had always hidden from myself by drinking until I couldn't hear myself screaming inside anymore.

Swadhyaya, when done without judgement, criticism or the editing that the conscious mind may want to encourage, can lead to some astonishing revelations as the subconscious reveals things it has always known but has not been able to tell us. There were many times when I was typing at my laptop, completely in flow with my writing, when I would suddenly sit back in astonishment at something I had just learned about myself after I typed it.

### Do you need to study Yoga to do this?

A lot of Swadhyaya relates to a deep study of Yoga, and of incorporating that study into daily life, thinking and meditating on what is learned through the Yoga study and taking steps on a daily basis to live a 'Yoga Life'. However, Self Study is accessible to all, and it is not necessary to embark on a lifelong deep study to gain some of the benefits of this practice.

## Begin with the Breath

As with everything in Yoga, Swadhyaya begins with the breath. Practice becoming aware of the breath, spend time focussing on the breath, work on deepening and slowing the breath whenever possible. Be aware of when your breath speeds up when you move faster or are stressed, and notice how long it takes to return to 'normal'.

## Developing Awareness

Become aware of your body, of how your body feels, of how you move your body, and start to notice and tend to the signals your body gives to tell you what you need. If you are tired, instead of overloading your body with coffee to keep going, maybe try to rest a little, or drink some water to hydrate yourself instead. This is particularly important when trying to defeat an addiction, as we often neglect our physical self-care when in the grip of addiction. I would keep drinking long after I should have gone to bed, never getting enough sleep, never listening to my body pleading with me to stop.

Develop awareness of the tremendous power the emotions hold over the physical wellbeing of the body. Negative emotions have a negative effect on the body, creating stress and tension that we can eliminate through awareness. Simple deep breaths, the old adage of 'take a deep breath and count to ten' can sometimes be all that is needed, sometimes maybe a longer count is called for. By gaining awareness of our emotions, we can learn to control our response to them, instead of letting them control our actions.

Awareness of the mind, and the effects the mind can have on the emotions, and in turn the body, can help to prevent the negative emotions developing. If the mind is allowed to dwell on a negative thought, this can all too quickly turn into a negative emotion. This is a very useful awareness to develop if trying to beat addiction. Cravings are, a lot of the time, entirely mental in their nature.

A useful 'mantra' to remember when dealing with cravings and stress is 'this shall pass', when you find yourself getting caught up in a worry or craving thought, try reminding yourself that it will pass, and distract yourself by focussing on your breath, or write about the thoughts to release them that way.

<u>Write it down, let it go</u>

Writing things down it a fantastic way to process thoughts and feelings, and to access parts of your mind you usually keep close. As I have said above, some of my greatest revelations when writing my coursework happened without the knowledge of my conscious mind at all, my subconscious mind was allowed to flow and it revealed its secrets to me.

A useful technique for this is 'Morning Pages'. I have started doing this a little, but am not doing it entirely properly. To really do this, you keep a notebook by your bed, and as soon as you wake (maybe going to the loo first!) you write 3 pages, without thinking too much about them, without editing, and without the intention to read them afterwards. This process allows the subconscious mind to 'let go' and release things you don't even know are in there!

This process of writing was fundamental to my recovery, but, it is important to note, I had support and people who I could talk to about this. I do not advise doing this unsupported if you are working through addiction recovery, make sure there is someone who knows what you are doing who can support you.

*20th February 2016, Ahimsa - non violence - our greatest strength?*
Yoga philosophy has much to teach us about the human condition, and how we can improve our lives.

We all want to be happy don't we, yet our lives are filled with things that make us unhappy. We are stressed at work, at home, in our relationships. We are told that buying things is the route to happiness, all the while knowing that consumption of these things is harming the very environment we depend on. We deal with our problems by numbing the feelings and hoping they will go away. We forget who we really are, and in the battle to get through life, we forget to live.

Why do we do this to ourselves? Can't we find a better way to live? One that brings joy, contentment, peace and happiness? Isn't that really ALL we want?

The ancient Yogic scriptures, the Yoga Sutras of Maharishi Patanjali, offers us an almost step by step guide to achieve contentment and happiness. It is NOT a quick fix, take this pill and all your problems will be over approach. The Eight Limbs of Yoga offer a routemap to 'Samadhi', or Enlightenment. It is a way to live that brings meaning, peace and happiness into life. As with all journeys in life, it is as much about the journey as the destination. Along the journey, the Eight Limbs gives us a path to create happy lives for ourselves, starting NOW.

Yoga is not just exercise and meditation, although these are aspects of the Eight Limbs (what chance do we have of happiness if we don't take care of our body and mind?). The foundations of a happy, healthy life according to these ancient writings are to be found in our behaviour and our approach to life.

The five Yamas are the 'moral restraints'. They tell us what we should not do if we want to live a good, happy life. They are:-

Ahimsa - non violence

Satya - truth

Asteya - non stealing

Brahmacharya - control of creative energy, restraint

Aparigraha - non posessiveness

Ahimsa - no harm

Ahimsa, at its most basic, means not hurting or harming. This does not just refer to others, but also to the harm we might do to ourselves as well. Ahimsa is not just about not harming other humans either; Yogic philosophy believes that the soul travels through many life forms on the way to becoming human, so we must not harm any life forms as the soul that resides in them is as important as the soul that lives in us.

Ahimsa reminds us that we are all connected, and that harm to one ultimately leads to harm to many. The great Mahatma Ghandi was a famous proponent of Ahimsa, his non violent revolution brought about huge change in India in the early 20th Century and was probably far more effective than if he had led a violent revolution

Non-violence is the greatest force at the disposal of mankind. It is mightier than the mightiest weapon of destruction devised by the ingenuity of man.

## Ahimsa and our thoughts

Ahimsa teaches us to take care of our thoughts about ourselves and others, to try to cease the negative and sometimes cruel self talk we subject ourselves to, and to refrain from passing judgement on others. Brene Brown, in 'The Power of Vulnerability' points out that when we judge others we are reflecting our own insecurities, so when we feel a need to judge others, this might be an invitation to look inwards and see how we can boost ourselves instead of putting others down.

Our thoughts create physical responses in our body. Negative thoughts have a negative effect on the body. We see that clearly in the face of someone who frowns a lot, as they age the frown lines on their face become more and more pronounced. Negativity reduces our immune system and creates a stress response, causing the body to produce stress hormones. If this feeling is maintained, the stress it creates can lead to a range of physical and mental health problems.

The opposite is true. A person who smiles a lot will have deep smile lines as they age, rather than frown lines. When we think happy thoughts our bodies respond accordingly, and the pleasure centre of the brain is activated, leading us to feel happier and boosting our physical health. Increasing scientific evidence shows that optimistic people recover better from illness than negative people.

## Ahimsa and our words

The words we use, as well as our thoughts, have a powerful effect on us and the people around us. The old schoolyard rhyme 'Sticks and stone will break my bones but words will never hurt me' is, to be quite frank, utterly nonsense. While physical hurt can be devastating, words can be equally destructive. I know I still carry scars of things said to me, or things I said which I regret, going back to my earliest memories. Words can hurt us deeply and can change the course of someone's life forever. Try to bring awareness into how you speak to yourself and others, and notice when you say things which make yourself or others uncomfortable.

## Ahimsa and our diet

Ahimsa encourages us to live in such a way which doesn't cause harm, either directly or indirectly to others. This very strongly suggests a vegetarian diet to many people. However, an insight into the dairy and egg industries suggests, or is did to me at least, that these vegetarian staples are far from non violent, and veganism seemed to be the only way to ensure Ahimsa in my diet. In his series of audio lectures, 'The Lost Teachings of Yoga' Georg Feuerstein refers to a 'strict vegetarian diet' as being one that does not involve eggs or dairy products', so maybe we have vegetarianism all wrong anyway. Veganism does not work for everyone, I know, so I am passing no judgement, simply sharing my experience.

There are, of course, other factors to take into account when trying to bring Ahimsa into the diet, and considerations such as farming methods and food transportation which harm the environment, trading methods which subject human workers to harsh conditions and insufficient pay, and packaging of processed food are all in some way harming others.

In the modern world it is impossible to eat in a fully ethical way unless you are able to live entirely on food you produce yourself, there is a great deal of harm inherent in our food system. So we all have to just make decisions based on what is right for us and our values system.

It is important that in we ensure that our body has all it needs to be healthy. We do this through eating good, nutritious food in moderation, ensuring we are adequately hydrated and trying to avoid excessive processed food. So many physical diseases that afflict us in the 21st century could be avoided, or minimised, if we all ate better. Chemicals in processed food, insufficient vitamins, too much fat, too much processed sugar...it all takes its toll on our health and well being.

Ahimsa in Yoga practice

Be at peace with yourself in your practice.

When you are on your Yoga mat, it is important that Ahimsa is your guiding light throughout. This means listening to your body, and, where possible, doing the practices that your body needs, and not doing the things that aren't right for you. If a certain posture causes pain, don't do it, or ask your teacher to suggest modifications at least. There should never be pain in yoga - yes, you should feel stretched, and yes, you should become aware of your muscles, but there should never be pain, pain means STOP. There is no 'pushing through the pain' in Yoga

Ahimsa in Yoga also means accepting your limits and not trying to push yourself beyond them for the sake of 'keeping up with others' So what if the person next to you can get their nose closer to their knees, or looks like a ballerina she is so graceful and elegant. That is her business, not yours, and it should not be the standard to which you hold yourself. Maybe she is a ballerina, maybe she has hypermobility syndrome and her flexibility causes her pain, you just don't know. Your yoga practice is just that, yours. It about your relationship with yourself, not how you compare to others. Once you can let go of the need to compare yourself to others in the class, you will find you enjoy your yoga practice so much more (this is true whether you are seeing yourself as 'better' or 'worse' than others in the class). Remember that it is the Ego that creates all these thoughts, and through regular Yoga practice you will learn to move away from the ego and be guided by your deeper Self, so don't give in to the demands of the Ego, allow the deeper Self to emerge through a gentle loving approach to your practice.

Any step we take towards living a life of Ahimsa will bring its own rewards. Please don't feel you are somehow failing if you can't change over night - no one can. It is a lifetime's work, and, as I said before, it is the journey, and what you learn about life and yourself along the way, that makes it all worthwhile, don't worry about the destination!

*27 March 2016, post in a Facebook group*
I'm writing a book. It is going to be a great book, the story of one woman's struggle with depression and addiction, and how she found salvation and sobriety through Yoga. It's going to include techniques the reader can use to help with various aspects of their own health and wellbeing. The Me I was a few years ago would LOVE to read this book myself, would really benefit from reading this book. I think it is her...me... that I am writing it for.

Except I'm not. Not really. I have got maybe about 18000 words between a couple of blog posts I know I can use, and a 22 page document I write in from time to time. I managed to stop myself from telling people I was 'trying' to write a book, and started saying I was writing a book, it felt good, but I haven't written anything in it for a while.

At the start of the month I joined a friend of mine in a 1000 words a day challenge. I did really well for the first few days. I got a couple of blog posts written, I wrote in my book, I was feeling great. Then the distractions started. At first it seemed completely acceptable – my eldest son was visiting, I hadn't seen him for months as he spends his life travelling around Europe. I spent a lot of time working on my business instead of being with him, there was a limit to what I wanted to prioritise over him. The book seemed to be a legitimate sacrifice.

After he left, I announced that I was 'back on the horse' and wrote one thing. Then there were more distractions. They just kept coming. Domestic crises, a weekend retreat, pain in my back that meant sitting at the laptop for any length of time was almost unbearable, my middle son coming to visit, working on a much overdue business plan – the distractions just kept on coming, and the procrastinating voices kept saying 'it's ok, you can do it tomorrow'

I love writing, when I am in a flow. Sometimes the words are simply waiting to pour out of me and it is all I can do to slow them down enough so I can keep up with them to write or type them out. This is when I write the stuff that makes ME cry, makes me sit back in shock at some revelation I have just had AFTER I TYPED IT, makes me so proud to hit that publish button, when I write material I want to read over and over again. Then I know I can write.

Other times I sit down to write and it feels like I am trying to give blood through a straw, the space for the words to pour into is so much bigger then the hole they can come out of, they are stuck. Often the words will be in my head right up to the point when I sit down to write them, then they go and hide in the shadows just before I can catch them. When this happens, I turn to a comfort habit, just as surely as I used to turn to wine when stressed.

Hello Facebook, hello pointless research, hello 'oh, I'll just wash the dishes', hello do anything but the task I sat down to do...hello Procrastination

I have come to the conclusion that I am probably addicted to procrastination. Characteristics of addiction include (to quote Gabor Mate).

1.      Compulsive engagement with the behaviour, a preoccupation with it

2.      Impaired control over the behaviour

3.      Persistence or relapse, despite evidence of harm

4.      Dissatisfaction or intense craving when the object is not immediately available

Apart from 4, I would say that all those characteristics apply to my procrastination. I work much better when procrastination is no readily available (eg, I work better on the train with no internet available).

The world offers us a million ways to procrastinate in our daily life, particularly when we are engaging with technology for the work we are doing. I don't know how many times I have absent mindedly opened Facebook when I had no intention of doing so! I can get side tracked by any 'shiny penny' that comes along. But it does me no end of harm. I have not got the 30000 words I should have written for my book. I don't have a load of decluttered items listed on ebay earning me money. I still haven't finished the many books I decided I was going to read this year. My procrastination brings me nothing but worry and panic when I realise it is either too late, or nearly too late, to get anything done.

Yet I try to control my procrastination. This is what joining Natasha's 1000 word challenge was all about. I tried, I did really well for a while, then I failed. This feels like a relapse. I tried to beat my procrastination and failed.

Whenever I tried to control my drinking or smoking in the past and failed my response would generally by 'ah well then, sod it, I may as well get pissed/smoke loads now'. I would see my failures as proof that I was never going to be free of my addiction and surrender to it a little more.

But now I know that I can beat addictions. If I can beat addictions I was using to hide from things I didn't like about my life, I am sure I can beat a procrastination addiction that is preventing me from accessing the things I DO want in life.

I have a choice here. I can either look at my failure to write this month as proof that I am not ever going to write a book, and spend the rest of my life feeling disappointed in myself that I didn't write, or I can get back on that damn horse and start writing again! I know which I would prefer…I've done the living with regret and disappointment for too many years, it doesn't fit me well. I have big dreams for my life and one of them is to see my name on the shelf in a book shop, so write I will. On 1 April I am going to start again, 1000 words a day, it isn't hard, I've done more than that now, starting at 10 past 1 in the morning!

April is going to be 'get back on the damn horse month, want to join me?

*(I didn't stick to the 1,000 words a day, but I did decide mid way through the month to get the book finished in time to launch in India in May!).*

# Disclaimer

While the author has used her best efforts in preparing this book, she makes no representations or warranties with respect to the accuracy or completeness of the contents of this book and specifically disclaims any implied warranties of merchantability or fitness for a particular purpose. The strategies contained herein may not be suitable for your situation. You should consult a professional where appropriate. The reader is aware of the fact that the advice herein is not to be construed as psychological counselling, medical advice or any other form of therapy or treatment.

Neither Author nor Publisher shall be held liable for any loss or damages, including, but not limited to, special, incidental, consequential or other damages. The reader takes full responsibility for the physiological, psychological, emotional, career and financial decisions that they may or may not make after reading as well as any consequences.

# Publication Details

Bent Back Into Shape, Beating Addiction Through Yoga

Published in the United Kingdom by Esther Nagle.

Createspace ISBN-13: 978-1539372844

First Edition: October 2016

Category: Non-Fiction / Personal Development

Made in the USA
Lexington, KY
31 October 2016